YUCATÁN COOKBOOK

Photo: Linda Seals

YUCATÁN
Cookbook

Recipes & Tales

Lyman Morton

RED CRANE   SANTA FE

First Edition
Printed in the United States of America
Photography by Michael O'Shaughnessy
Food Stylist: Kathi Long
Cover art by Jorge Rosano
Cover and book design by Linda Seals/B.Vader Design

Library of Congress Cataloging-in-Publication Data
Morton, Lyman, 1943–
        Yucatán Cookbook : recipes and tales / Lyman Morton.
            p.   cm.
        Includes index.
        ISBN 1-878610-51-1
            1. Cookery, Mexican.   2. Cookery—Mexico—Yucatán (state)
    3. Yucatán (Mexico : State)—Description and travel.   I. Title.
        TX716.M4M67   1996
        641.5972'65—dc20
                                                                        96-1978
                                                                        CIP

Permission to quote from *Witch Doctor* by Ross Bagdasarian © 1958, Monarch Music

Red Crane Books, Inc.
2008-B Rosina Street, Suite B
Santa Fe, New Mexico 87505

Contents

*To the memory of Vanesa Moreno, who handled kitchenware with a
delicacy and grace that brought to mind musician, surgeon, or mother.*

Acknowledgments

I cannot imagine having written this book without the help of Alberto
Castillo, a Yucatecan who patiently and knowledgeably answered hundreds of my questions. I also wish to give special thanks to Petra Varney
of Chelem for her help and patience; to Doña María, Manuela, and the
entire Estrella family for their hospitality and sharing of recipes; and to
Martha Nava for her help and entertainment.

I want to thank the many waiters and cooks, both in restaurants
and at home, who were happy to share their knowledge of food and cooking. Most of the time I did not know their names. Some exceptions are:
Carlos, owner of Il Petite Great Restaurant Deus Mexico in Mérida;
Umberto Aldecua, owner of El Alacrán restaurant in Dzilam de Bravo;
Otilio Estrada of Dzilam de Bravo, who claimed that dead men came to
eat his seafood soup; Cheto, owner of the La Cueva de Macumba in Río
Largatos; Doña Tina, owner of Doña Tina's Cocina Economica in Tulum;
and Javier Mimenza, owner of Los Flamboyanes in Mérida.

Not least, I want to thank Michael and Marianne O'Shaughnessy of
Red Crane Books for their interest in a Yucatán cookbook.

THE YUCATÁN

GULF OF ME

Veracruz

V E R A C
R
U
Z

T A B

Oaxaca

O A X A C A

C H I

Dzilam de Bravo

Dzidzantún

Progresso
Chelem

Temax

Mérida

Izamal

Celestún

Huhí

Valladolid

Chichén Itzá

Cancún

Y U C A T Á N

X I C O

C A M P E C H E

Campeche

Q U I N T A N A   R O O

Campotón

A S O

C O

Palenque

G U A T E M A L A

A P A S

Introduction

My earliest memories of Mexico came shortly after World War II and well before I knew what a taco was. The only thing I remember on the trip was my father scaring me on the Pacific Coast Highway by saying, "Okay, I'm going to drive into the water now," everytime the highway got close to the ocean. I half believed him. I was in my fourth year, but some of the things that I remember about Tijuana had little to do with him.

I saw Mexican jumping beans and wondered why they jumped. I have since learned that the seeds of tropical shrubs belonging to the spurge family become infested with the larvae of a small moth. The larvae within will move, causing the seed to roll from side to side, flip over endwise, or actually jump.

Aside from these memories, I was left with vague impressions of dirt streets, burros, big hats, and the feeling that this place was different from any that I had known. Perhaps a slight apprehension I felt from my mother helped convey that feeling. I don't remember my father being that way. He was quite brave. After all, he had been about to drive into the Pacific Ocean.

Most of my early impressions of Mexico came from Hollywood. After seeing reruns decades later, I realized that my father had taken us to Humphrey Bogart movies as well as to Tijuana. Two scenes had stood out in my mind all these years. One was Humphrey Bogart shooting Edward G. Robinson on a yacht in *Key Largo.* The other was Bogart telling a Mexican *bandido,* "Get away from my burro," just before being slain himself in *Treasure of Sierra Madre.* Through movie portrayals I came to think of Mexico as a place teeming with bandits, dirt streets, burros, and sultry women dancing in smoky adobe bars.

The movie *One-Eyed Jacks* with Marlon Brando added a new dimension to the Mexico in my mind. Seeing the pretty coastal scenes, I came to think of Mexico as a place with great spans of coast and an abundance of fresh seafood. I liked the idea of Mexico long before coming to know it firsthand.

Border Crossings

While moving from my home in Georgia to California in 1967, I drove along a small road I had spotted on a map the night before. It paralleled

Interstate 10 near El Paso, Texas, and was closer to the border. Seeing an occasional light in the distance, I thought, "That light is in Mexico. If I were standing next to that light, I'd be in Mexico." It was exactly where I wanted to be.

Until then I hadn't realized how fascinated I was with the country, how romantic it was to me. My idea of Mexico was like going back in time: inexpensive, no fast foods or TV dinners or supermarkets, people living without televisions, and freedom to drive as one wished, unrestrained by dictates of the state or the whims of police officers. It was in a Mexican restaurant along this stretch of road that I learned what a taco and an enchilada look like. This seems hard to believe, such has been the spread of Mexican food throughout much of the world since 1967.

After settling down in California, I spent many summers exploring Mexico. Crossing the border was always exciting, like an amusement park would be to some. *Bang,* there you were in a different culture! Boarding an airplane and landing on another continent is not nearly as striking as walking across the United States-Mexican border into Tijuana, or Juárez, or any other border town. The tacky towns on the United States side of this great divide give only a hint of what life is like on the other side.

The smells are suddenly different: *carne asada* (roast meat) filling the air like a backyard barbecue, tortillas and a variety of meats frying in grease, exhaust fumes, an occasional waft of garbage. The places of business are different too. Auto upholstery shops sit beside art and craft vendors, taco stands and marriage/divorce places with signs that seem to offer package deals. Buildings, even one-room shacks, are painted in gaudy colors—bright yellows, turquoise, pinks.

Rules of the road are similar to those in the United States, but only on paper. In practice, stop signs become yield signs. And drivers retain the right to create a lane for traffic wherever they desire, as long as it is to the right of center. Strangely, people lose their lead feet when they leave the city and get out on the open road. In the city, one must drive either defensively or get into the spirit of the competition and be aggresive. In the country, just the opposite is true. Drivers are apt to be moving along very slowly.

This relationship to the road is one of a plethora of paradoxes exhibited by the Mexican people. Another is that although both drivers and pedestrians can be rude while waiting their turn, *"Mi casa, tu casa"* reigns supreme. Still another is that a large percentage of men intent on demonstrating their masculinity also take pride in their knowledge of cooking.

The vehicles, like the feats they perform, are also different south of the border. Noisy, smoky, beat-up buses clatter along, their drivers surrounded by garish decorations—if not a picture of Jesus or Mary, then often a Disneyland-type sign emblazoned with the head of Mickey Mouse. Cars are frequently painted in three or more colors, with no symmetry to their schemes, and they are likely to move along like crabs because their frames have been bent and always will be. A large number of cars break down on the road. In the north, a Tecate can capped with a rock—two easy roadside finds—will be placed about fifty yards behind a disabled vehicle, serving as a flare. Farther south, several rocks or a small branch of a tree is more common. For good reason, a road sign seen throughout Mexico reminds drivers, "Don't leave stones on the road."

I once saw five trucks turned over in a two-day period. People then stand around guarding what is not wrecked until help arrives. I have the idea that a broken-down car car does not cause as much unhappiness as it does in the United States. *Así es la vida* ("Such is life"), the owner will say, palms turned upward.

I liked this bombardment of the senses that occurred each time I crossed the border, and the *qué será* attitude that applied to more than the romance, looks, and wealth that Doris Day sang about.

For me one of the enjoyments of being in a foreign country is to try new things to eat and drink and experience the atmosphere in the cafés and bars. Something I immediately noticed in Mexico was that people in the *loncherias* were eating foods I did not recognize, dishes not served in Southern California's Mexican restaurants.

A hog has a reputation for several undesirable traits, among them gluttony. Although he takes the brunt of the insults, other quadrapeds usually have their snouts to the ground also, preoccupied with getting a bite to eat. While many of us people have other concerns as well, a significant amount of thought goes into what we are going to feed ourselves. I know people in the United States who would rather read a cookbook than a novel. And in Mexico, it is easier to have a conversation about food than even sex. We, like the hogs, have a wide variety of tastes. We will eat anything. Everywhere in Mexico I found new things to eat and new ways to prepare the familiar.

The Yucatán Peninsula

One thing that originally drew me to the Yucatán was simply the knowledge that this peninsula was as far as one could go in Mexico and that meandering through the country to get there would have a magical quality to it. As it turned out, being there did too, for the Yucatán has a charm of its own. Until the mid-twentieth century, the peninsula was all but isolated from the rest of Mexico and was accessible primarily by sea. Indeed, residents in the capital city of Mérida had more contact with Europeans than with other Mexicans.

In recent years, of course, "Yucatán" has become a household word in the United States. It entered the lexicon on the heels of increased interest in Maya ruins, the flocking of tourists to the Caribbean coastal resort of Cancún built nearly twenty-five years ago on virgin beaches, and cable television's "world weather" reports of hurricanes in the region. My first trip into the area was in 1972 when Cancún was still a tiny, remote fishing village not even shown on maps.

I have always felt that entering the Yucatán from southern Mexico is like slipping into yet another country. The animals crossing the highway are different—instead of cows and burros, one sees furry ant-eating creatures, *tejóns* (small fruit-eating animals with bulbous noses), and white-faced animals called *perros del monte*. Even the raccoons and opossums have different coloring from those I have seen anywhere else.

Road signs announcing, *"No Estacionarse en Curva"* ("Do Not Park in Curve") are common, as are bicycles and *triciclos* (large tricycles with platforms on the front for hauling small objects) pedaled along the highway at night without so much as a reflector. For Yucatec Maya villagers, the second half of the twentieth century may have come too quickly.

Here villages are known as "pueblos," and their names are often Maya words beginning with the letter "X"—pronounced "sh"—or composed of seemingly unpronounceable letter combinations such as "xk" or "tz." Most of the pueblos look alike. Rough stone walls line the streets and beside them grow *flamboyanes*, beautiful trees whose wide-spreading branches bloom with bright red flowers. Dotting the outskirts of each pueblo are native stick-and-stucco oval houses with *chosas* (palm roofs). Soon the indigenous huts give way to buildings reflective of the Hispanic occupation of the region, which dates back to the mid-sixteenth century.

In this sector of the village, one is likely to see, in addition to a small Fundamentalist church and an Alcoholico Anonimo, an occasional store, a part-time restaurant, a cantina, and a billiard parlor. The central square is invariably flanked by a municipal building on one side and a Catholic church—the largest structure in town—on the other.

The pueblos are neat by south-of-the-border standards, perhaps because, unlike so many Mexican towns, they are not dominated by concrete blocks and rebar. In fact, ruins of old buildings are far more prominent than half-finished abandoned ones.

Driving numerous times from California to Mérida, I would pass through all three of the peninsula's states: Campeche on the west, Quintana Roo on the east, and Yucatán, the northernmost home of the Yucatec Maya. In none of this country, aside from the beach resorts and the run-down houses on the north Yucatán coast, do signs of human habitation detract from the beauty of the terrain. To the contrary, the stone walls, haciendas, ancient pyramids, and even colonial Mérida enhance the landscape.

The land between the pueblos surrounding Mérida was once cultivated. Today, rock walls encircle abandoned *henequén* fields reclaimed by wild tropical growth. *Henequén* plants, now wild themselves, are scattered here and there. Crossing the road at irregular intervals are tiny railroad tracks for donkey-drawn carts that hauled the sword-like leaves from the fields for processing and drying into sisal fiber. Every now and then one can see a field that is still cultivated, its *henequén* plants standing in rows for hundreds of yards. They are an anachronism, a throwback to pre-World War II years when synthetic rope fibers were not yet mass produced and the Yucatán was the rope-producing capital of the world. More often, one sees a crumbling *henequén* hacienda and beside it a smokestack protruding from a thick growth of trees. The rainforest quickly overtakes things, as it has done with the ancient Maya ruins.

Yucatán cooking, I'm happy to say, is one regional treasure that has not been lost to the passage of time. Culinary influences date back beyond remembrance, as generations of sons and daughters passed on recipes they learned from their parents. Wild turkey, deer, and *jabalí* (a type of wild pig) are indigenous to the Yucatán. Corn, tomatoes, cocoa, avocados, bananas, squash, potatoes, yams, *frijoles*, *achiote*, chiles, and *epazote* were used in the Yucatán before the Spanish conquest. *(Epazote* also grows wild in many parts of the United States, where it is known as pigweed, goosefoot, wormseed, or ironweed.) Many other ingredients now used in Yucatán cooking arrived with Spanish settlers in the sixteenth century and became popularized after the Spanish conquest. Most notable among these imports are garlic, onion, wheat, vinegar, lard, pepper, cumin, oregano, cinnamon, sugarcane, garbanzos, pork, beef, rice, olive oil, mutton, and limes. The Spanish also brought pigs, cows, beasts of burden, and disease.

Today's distinctive style of Yucatán cooking is found primarily in small restaurants, *cocinas económicas,* and the homes of native people. Most of the cooking utensils used in the Yucatec Maya kitchen are ubiquitous throughout Mexico. Common items include a three-legged stone *molcajete* (sometimes called a *tamolad*) for grinding, a small wooden *molcajete* for mixing chile sauces, an iron *comal* (or griddle) for cooking and warming tortillas, a *lec* (a gourd) used to keep tortillas warm, a *jícara* (a gourd) used as a mug to hold liquid, a large steamer for cooking *al vapor* or *en baño de María,* pots larger than those typically used in North American homes, plus knives, forks, spoons, and plenty of hands.

Sometimes a long-handled steel utensil with holes in the bottom is used to mash cooked *frijoles,* though more often they are mashed with a large spoon. At times a lime squeezer is used, although usually the juice is extracted by doubling a wedge of lime over the dull edge of a knife. And although a tortilla press can be found occasionally, most people who make their own tortillas do so by hand.

In the pueblos, many *indígenas* still have a *metate* and *metlapil.* A *metate* is a slightly concave slab of rock about one foot wide by one and one-half feet long. Composed of the same black stone as a *molcajete,* it slants downward on its three legs. The *metate* and *metlapil,* a roller also made of this stone, are used in the grinding of *maiz* (corn) for tortillas and *atole.* Many pueblo households also have a traditional *banqueta* and *banquillo*—a small wooden table and stool for the person mixing the *masa* (ground corn) to make tortillas.

When visiting people's homes and dining at restaurants, I often ended up in the kitchen collecting recipes. Even in cantinas and night clubs, conversations would turn to *la comida Yucateca.* People everywhere were happy to share their recipes and their knowledge of cooking, for Yucatecans are extremely proud of their heritage.

The biggest problems I had gathering recipes had to do with measuring and timing. "How much?" I would ask, and "How long?" After some peculiar stares, I was either shown quantities by the shaping of a hand or given some Spanish equivalent of "Until it is done," accompanied by a shrug and raised eyebrows, as though I had just arrived from another planet. Measuring devices and timers, I was to learn, are not normally used in Yucatecan cooking, not even for rice.

Moving to Mexico

In 1994, I finally did what I had thought of doing for eleven years: I moved to the Yucatán for an indefinite period of time, for as long as I wanted to stay. It is not easy to uproot oneself from a house that has been home for eighteen years—in my case, a sanctuary in the greater Los Angeles area—after packing up all of life's necessities and a lot of its material junk. It is nothing like going away for the summer.

There was little sadness when I finally left Los Angeles in my filled-to-the-gills Toyota pickup, pulling a 600 cc Honda Trans-Alp motorcycle on a small trailer and leaving as behind schedule as a Mexican train's arrival in the rainy season. I felt more excitement than apprehension as I took the long drive out of the Los Angeles basin, for I had no clear idea of my destination other than some new place to call home in or near Mérida. Most of all, I was curious. I would be wending my way down the Pacific coast of Mexico, then heading north into the Yucatán. In short, I knew one thing—this was the beginning of a vacation for the rest of my life. *Qué será será.*

A few miles south of the border crossing at Nogales, Arizona, I stopped to have my tourist card signed and stamped and to get permission for me and my vehicles to be in Mexico. Customs procedures had changed since my previous visit: entering Mexico had become computerized and a major credit card was now required of anyone bringing a vehicle into the country. After waiting in three or four line-like configurations, I was almost free of red tape. Things were going as well as could be expected, and all that remained was a token inspection of my belongings.

As it turned out, I had so much stuff that they did not even bother to go through it. When asked what was in the back of the truck, however, I made the mistake of mentioning my outboard motor. The scene that followed was reminiscent of precomputerized Mexico. Apparently, you can put computers in Mexico, but you cannot take the blood out of its people.

The customs official said I would have to go back to the Maritime Customs Office in Nogales, which had closed for the day. It was okay to bring a boat and motor into Mexico, he told me, but to bring a motor by itself would cost twenty percent of its value.

"But I told the inspector at the border about the motor, and he said to go on," I replied trying to look forlorn and finding it easy.

He would talk to his superior, he said.

Immediately, uniformed men began to gather at the back of my truck. *El Jefe* (the chief) told me that maybe for fifty dollars he would turn his head and that fifty dollars is less than the amount I would have to pay in Nogales. Another official climbed on my motorcycle and asked if he could buy it. To change the focus, I handed a third officer a couple of *Playboy* magazines I had brought along. (Before leaving, I had tossed eight old *Playboys* and a *Hustler* into my truck for just such a purpose.)

One of the officials saw that I had more and demanded them all, saying. *"¿Es pornografía,si? ¡No pornografía en Mexico!"* He spoke in a happy tone, a smile on his face.

They took the magazines, excited and laughing. I thought of elementary school children when the substitute teacher has brought a treat. El Jefe wrote on my permission slip: "9.9 horsepower Mercury." *"No problema*—my outboard motor was legally admitted into Mexico, and nothing more was said about money. What was said as they looked through the issue of *Hustler* I will never know, though it must have sparked some good laughs.

Driving down Mexico's Pacific coast in May was disappointing. I had been accustomed to the lush greens of summer after the rains had fallen. But alas, rainy season had not yet started. Once pretty rivers were dry. Most of the vegetation was parched and dusty. Hundreds of small fires burned along the roadside. Some appeared to have been started intentionally to prepare the fields for planting. Most did not. Lit cigarettes were frequently tossed out the windows of passing cars and trucks.

The roads seemed rougher than ever before and there were even more *topes* (speed bumps) than I had remembered. Previously peaceful cities were crowded and noisy, and the traffic was abominable. Buses and trucks with their cut-out exhausts climbed the hills in first gear, stringing behind them long streams of bumper-to-bumper vehicles.

The beauty of the open road, that wonderful feeling of freedom it brings still exists, but not nearly everywhere, as it did just a few years ago.

Travel books about Mexico have always warned tourists not to drive at night because of the cows and burros wandering about on the roads. I had a friend who considered a Mexican cow at night worse than anything the old Soviet Union would have pointed at a United States soldier. I never understood this fear. I figured that as long as a driver is furnished with pedals to regulate speed, brakes, and headlights and a brain to call upon, what is the problem? On this trip though, for the first time, local people cautioned me against driving at night, especially alone. It was not quadrupeds they were warning me about—it was thieves. Several truck drivers outside of Chihuahua explicitly advised me to look out for *los ladrónes* (robbers) on the road from Durango to Mazatlán at night. "You will be safe if you leave Durango by eleven in the morning," they told me.

I began to wonder: Had I left a world of drive-bys for one of highwaymen?

I left Durango by eleven in the morning, made it safely to Mazatlán, and kept going down the coast. About seventy miles south of Manzanillo, I noticed a weathered sign that read, *"Playa—2 Km."* Turning onto a narrow road, I drove the two kilometers and arrived at a ranch on the beach. Before me were two large *palapas* with tables and chairs. An old man was resting in a hammock while his wife scurried about, performing endless chores. They were the owners of the ranch and its nameless restaurant. The man told me that the road here, too, was dangerous after dark, that the robbers "go to work" at eight o'clock each night. He invited me to spend the evening with his family and leave in the morning.

Juan, one of his sons, sat with me and chatted. He and his brother, he said, would be glad to have me join them at a Cinco de Mayo celebration that evening. There would be wild-bull riding, cock fights, and of course a *baile* (dance). Come Cinco de Mayo, he said, there is always a *baile*. I accompanied them to the festivities and spent the night at their parents' house on the beach.

As I was leaving in the morning, the old man invited me to stay anytime I happened to be passing by. The entire family had welcomed me graciously, as is often the case in Mexico.

My spirits had improved significantly by the time I reached the state of Oaxaca. So, too, had the roads. Traffic dwindled to practically nothing, and the indigenous Oaxaqueña style of cooking was in the air.

Still, the rains had not come and the pretty rivers flowing into the ocean that I had remembered in Guerrero and Oaxaca were dry.

By the time I arrived in Puerto Escondido, I had been in thirteen different places the previous thirteen nights. I saw a place I had never noticed before, Bungalows El Marinero. It was perfect: off the highway and a two-minute walk to the ocean. It had a gate that was locked at night and each bungalow was provided a parking space. A pretty girl was sitting on the step of what appeared to be the only occupied one.

The proprietress, after assuring me that my motorcycle would be safe at her establishment, showed me to the corner room. The ocean was audible. The girl was two doors away. "She's a pretty girl from Argentina, very nice. She's alone. She's always alone," the owner told me.

"I'll take it," I replied.

By morning I had decided to stay another night. While paying for the room, I asked the owner if she ever cooked iguana. Occasionally, she said. She did not eat iguana; they are too ugly for her. But when her husband wants iguana, she sends a boy out to catch one. She then told me how to cook them. She said they had to be put over a fire for one-half hour or more. You have to burn them to get the skin off. She pretended to pull with her hands; it looked like she was pulling hard. Then the meat had to be boiled and the next layer of skin peeled off that would reveal the pure white meat that is considered a delicacy.

I was lying on my hammock late that afternoon when a boy came up and handed me the recipe. I was taken aback—not only by the prompt service but also by the fact that this woman, unlike most of the restaurant cooks I had met in Oaxaca, could write.

The girl from Argentina had just returned from the beach when the iguana recipe arrived. I told her what I had been given, and she came over to look at it. She was not quite sure what an iguana was, so I tried to describe it. When she understood, she said she would like to try it. I invited her into my kitchenette for a glass of wine, and we talked until midnight.

She told me her name was Gisela (pronounced Shi-SELL-a). Her accent was strange to me because she was from Argentina. She pronounced the letters "y" and "ll" as "sh." As a result, *"Allá en la playa"* ("There on the beach") became "Asha en la plasha." And, of course, a chicken was a "posho" and a horse a "cabasho." With my limited Spanish, I could not understand half of what she said, but it did not matter. Her melodious voice did not require intelligible words.

The following morning, Gisela accepted an invitation to accompany me to a lagoon about an hour's drive away. Before leaving, I went down to the beach to buy a fish from one of the boats that had just come in. After selecting the perfect fish, I cleaned it; basted it with olive oil; added salt, thyme, lime juice, and jalapeño slices; and wrapped it in aluminum foil. Then I put olive oil on two potatoes and wrapped them as well. The potatoes, which required a great deal of heat, went on the pipes from the manifold on my engine. The fish went on the valve cover for slow cooking. The throttle cable was ideal for holding down the tail of the fish while the smog-device hose anchored its head. I did not tell Gisela about any of this; I wanted to surprise her with a picnic.

After about half an hour of driving, Gisela said, "I keep smelling something good, like fish cooking. I thought it was coming from that little town, but I smell it now."

I told her there was a fish cooking on the engine.

"¡Linda!" ("Beautiful!") she said, smiling. "In that little town back there I thought everyone was cooking fish. Now, I'm looking for a house and I don't see one!"

A few minutes later, I stopped to turn the potatoes and adjust the fish. When we arrived at our destination, they were just right. And they were delicious.

Gisela also liked to cook. She had been in Puerto Escondido a couple of weeks before I arrived and had gone lobster fishing. She was fond of preparing lobster *al mojo de ajo* (lobster with garlic) (p. 200).

My stay in Puerto Escondido lasted two weeks and completely changed the nature of my trip to Mérida. I had driven 3500 miles and there was a long way to go, but it was no longer a chore. Being in Mexico was fun again. With 3500 miles behind me, I began looking forward to the long stretches of road that lay ahead.

From Puerto Escondido I passed through Tehuantepec, San Cristobal de las Casas, then north to Palenque. The ruins at Palenque were the first Maya ruins that I had ever seen.

Twenty-two years earlier, I had gazed at the Temple of Inscriptions pyramid from the parking lot. Gray and splendid, more than 1300 years old and sitting at the base of a jungle-covered mountain, it had given me chills. There were many others enjoying the same thing. I was more idealistic in those days and had been led to think by the travel writers that they had all but discovered these ruins. Surrounded by other travelers, I realized this was not the case.

The road from Palenque to Mérida is straight and flat and passes through miles of marshland. This long stretch of soft, wet land is one reason the Yucatán did not have much contact with the rest of Mexico. A good road was not completed until the mid-twentieth century. Although an occasional curve would have been welcome, I was repeatedly relieved of my boredom by the sight of beautiful, large marsh birds.

It was at Champotón, Campeche, where the Río Champotón meets the Gulf of Mexico, that I spent my last night on the road. In the early morning I watched the fishing boats come in and unload large *huachinango* (red snapper). They were bound, I was told, for the United States and Mexico City. It did not seem fair. In front of the market across the street, people were eating breakfast. Strangely, (it seemed to me) most of these early morning diners were having *sopa de menudencia,* chicken-foot soup. There were small fish and oysters in the market, but not the big snapper. Locals can only watch them come in and go out.

At last, after a nearly 5000-mile journey from Los Angeles, I pulled into Mérida and checked into a motel. As I was unhitching the motorcycle trailer to move it into the parking area beside my truck, a violent rainstorm broke loose. A man in the parking lot told me this was the first storm of the year. After all that distance, I had missed getting drenched by less than one minute. The rainy season had begun.

BOTANAS

The midday eating of *botanas* in restaurant-bars and cantinas has long been a tradition in the Yucatán. In some restaurants several plates of food will be served when a drink is ordered. What is thought of as a *botana* can be arbitrary. Some small towns serve what can be thought of as a dinner or *comida*, but in smaller portions. This list of foods are commonly thought of as *botanas*.

Quesadillas con Flor de Calabazas

Quesadillas with Squash Blossoms

1 or 2 squash blossoms for each tortilla
Oil or butter
About 2 tablespoons grated Oaxaca cheese for each tortilla (15.4 grams)
Corn tortillas

Remove the stems from the squash flowers and sauté about a minute on each side in just enough oil to cover the bottom of a frying pan.

Sprinkle cheese over half of the tortilla, and put the squash flower on top.

Fold over and cook on each side until cheese melts but is not oozing out.

Quesadillas con Cáscaras de Papas y Epazote

Quesadillas with Potato Skins and Epazote

Epazote is a "weed" used extensively for recipes in southern Mexican cooking. It grows in several varieties and has several names in the United States—goosefoot, Jerusalem oak, pazote, and pigweed. It can be bought dried in some markets. It supposedly has medicinal properties. One is fighting parasites; the other is combating gas from eating frijoles. Perhaps the ancient people discovered this. It is normal in the south to eat epazote with frijoles.

Put potato peels, chile, butter, and epazote in salted water to cover. Simmer until the water cooks down and the peels are tender. Fold all the above ingredients into the potato skin and fry in a small amount of oil, turning until tortilla is golden.

Potato skins, about one potato for each tortilla (cutting the peels off the potatoes requires some practice)
Jalapeño chiles, seeded and chopped (about ¼ for each tortilla)
1 branch epazote
Salt
Oil
Water

Tacos de Chapulines

Grasshopper Tacos

½ pound grasshoppers
    (¼ kilo)
8-10 chiles pasillas
8 cloves garlic, peeled
¼ pound butter (⅛ kg,
    112 g)
Salt
Tortillas
2 limes

Put grasshoppers in boiling water 2 minutes until they are completely dead. Rinse and dry. Pull off the wings, antennae, and legs, if desired.

Prepare the chiles as in recipe for iguana, and grind with the garlic. Fry in half the butter for 5 minutes. Add a little water from the soaked chiles to make a sauce if necessary.

Fry the grasshoppers in half the butter and salt for about 8 minutes.

Heat the tortillas in a dry pan or over an open flame.

Put some grasshoppers and chile sauce in each tortilla and roll.

Panuchos

Turkey Tostadas filled with Black Beans

Panuchos are made with tortillas that are still warm. Using your finger or a knife, open each tortilla along its upper edge and loosen a small portion of the thin top layer (the *hollejo*). Spread mashed black beans inside. Cover the bottom of a pan with enough cooking oil to cover tortillas, and fry the filled tortillas (on both sides) until slightly crisp. Drain on a paper towel, if desired.

On top of each tortilla place a layer of shredded chicken or turkey, preferably en escabeche, and a layer of pickled red onion slices. In lieu of the chicken, turkey, shark, beef or pork, hard boiled eggs may be used. Top, if you wish, with Xni Pec—a mixture of chopped tomato, onion, serrano chile, and cilantro, all mixed in sour orange juice.

Tortillas
Black beans, cooked and mashed
Chicken or turkey, cooked and shredded; cazon (shark), fried and shredded; beef or pork, cooked or ground; or eggs, hard-boiled and chopped
Pickled red onion slices
Paper towels (optional)
1 recipe Xni Pec (optional)

Salbutes

Turkey Tostadas

Salbutes are similar to panuchos, except the beans are omitted and, depending on who one talks to, the tortillas must be made "from scratch."

Papadzules

Tacos with Squash Seed Sauce

2 pounds (1 kg) tomatoes
1 sprig epazote
Habanero chiles to taste
Salt
4 tablespoons (56 ml)
    cooking oil
1 pound (450 g) squash
    seeds
15-20 tortillas
1 dozen eggs, hard-boiled
    and mashed with a fork

The topping for this botana calls for quite a lot of work. To cut down on preparation time, squash seed paste, available in many markets, can be used in lieu of the first six ingredients.

Boil the tomatoes with the epazote and habanero chiles in 1 quart (900 ml) salted water for 15 minutes. Remove the seed pulp from the tomatoes, and blend it with the chiles. Fry the mixture in 2 tablespoons (28 ml) oil until it forms a sauce.

Toast the squash seeds and grind them with the epazote together with a little water from the boiled tomatoes. Remove the oil that forms, saving it for later. Add a little water to the seed paste, and stir until it thickens (yet remains thin enough to pour).

Heat the tortillas in the remaining 2 tbsp. (28 ml) oil for a few seconds; more oil may be needed. Place some hard-boiled egg on each tortilla, and roll it up. Spoon the squash seed sauce over the top, followed by the tomato sauce, then the oil from the epazote and squash seeds.

Papas con Orejas

Cold Potatoes with Pigs Ears

Boil potatoes until tender. Peel and chop.

Burn hairs from ears (in the U.S. pigs ears are likely to be hairless), and boil until done in salted water. Chop.

Mix everything together with juice from sour orange. Serve cold.

12 potatoes
½ pound (225 g) pigs ears
1 onion, finely chopped
2 tablespoons chopped cilantro (6.2 g)
Habanero chiles al gusto, chopped
1 sour orange
Salt and pepper

Pezuñas Rebozadas

Batter Fried Pigs Feet

Put onion to marinate in salt, pepper, and juice from sour orange or vinegar.

Boil pigs feet in water with salt, oregano, and garlic until done, about 2 hours. Let cool and remove big bones that have no meat. Pull apart into pieces.

Separate eggs. Beat whites and yolks separately, then mix.

Add salt and pepper to flour. Dip pieces of meat in the eggs and then the flour. Fry in a little oil until golden.

Serve with marinated onion on top.

1 large onion, chopped
Salt
Pepper
Sour orange or vinegar
2 pounds (1 kg) pig feet
½ teaspoon (.3 gr) oregano
2 cloves garlic
3 eggs
Flour
Oil

Sopa de Almefas Secas

Clam Soup (Dry)

11 pounds (5 kg) clams
Oil
2 tomatoes
6 cloves garlic, minced
1 bell pepper, chopped
6 or 7 bay leaves
1-1½ teaspoon (5 gr) pepper
2 cups (386 g) rice
Salt

Open clams and save juice.

Fry all the other ingredients except rice for about 8 minutes.

Add rice and clam juice, "vitamins" he called it. Cover and simmer until rice is nearly done. Add water if necessary.

Add clams and cook until rice is done.

For soup or "wet," as he called it, use 1 cup (193 g) rice, at most, and add 12 ounces (336 ml) tomato sauce. This recipe can be served as a botana or a soup. Serves 10.

Croquetas de Pescado

Fish Croquettes

Sauté the onion in the butter until it's transparent.

Remove from fire and stir in the flour. Add the curry powder, and gradually add the milk, stirring over a low fire until it's smooth and thick.

Mix the fish and parsley into the white sauce. Allow to cool.

Make oblong croquettes with fish mixture about the size of a large lemon.

Heat oil in frying pan (about ⅓-inch, 1 cm deep).

Roll croquettes in flour, egg, breadcrumbs, or cornmeal, and fry, turning, until they are evenly brown.

½ onion, finely chopped
3 tablespoons (45 g) butter
5 tablespoons (75 g) flour
1 teaspoon (2.3 g) curry powder
1 cup (224 ml) milk
2 cups (284 g) finely shredded boiled fish
3 tablespoons (12 g) finely chopped parsley
Oil
Flour
1 egg, beaten
Breadcrumbs or cornmeal
Salt

Arroz con chivitas de Holbox

Rice with Conch from Holbox

3 tomatoes
½ small onion
3 tablespoons (10 g)
   cilantro leaves
1 clove garlic
1 tablespoons (15 g)
   margarine or butter
3 cups (579 g) rice
2 tablespoons (28 ml) oil
8 serrano chiles
½ bell pepper, or 1 chile
   dulce
1 pound (½ kg) chivitas
   (or conch meat)
2 teaspoons (1 g) pow-
   dered chicken bouillon

Chivitas are small conch-like creatures that are plentiful along the north coast of the Yucatán peninsula. Holbox is an island with a small fishing town just off the coast near the border of the states of Yucatán and Quintana Roo.

Conch could be substituted for chivitas in this recipe.

Blend tomatoes, onion, cilantro, and garlic, and strain.

Sauté in margarine about 15 minutes.

Fry rice in oil until it begins to turn golden, and add to tomato mixture.

Add chiles, 6 cups (1440 ml) water, chivitas. Cover and simmer until rice is done. Some forms of conch need to be boiled separately.

Sardinas en Chile Chipotle con Col en Ajonjolí

Sardines in Chile Chipotle with Sesame Cabbage

Roughly clean the sardines of skin and bones.

Blend the tomatoes, onion, and garlic with the beer and strain.

Fry the bacon and sardines in oil until they brown.

Add the potatoes, carrots, and peas, and fry 2 minutes or so.

Add the tomato and chile, cover, and cook over a slow flame, stirring from time to time until it becomes thick. Serve with *Col en Ajonjolí* which follows.

1 can of sardines (a can of tuna may be substituted)
2 tomatoes
½ onion
1-2 cloves garlic
¼ can beer
2 strips bacon, finely chopped
2 tablespoons (28 ml) oil
2 large potatoes, finely chopped
2 carrots, finely chopped
⅔ cup (100 g) canned peas
4 canned chipotle chiles, crushed (*al gusto*)

Col en Ajonjolí

Sesame Cabbage

Cabbage
2 eggs
Flour
1 teaspoon (5 g) sesame
   seeds
Oil
1 tablespoon (15 g) butter
Salt

Cut cabbage leaves into thirds.

Dip in eggs beaten with salt.

Dip in flour that has been mixed with sesame seeds.

Fry in oil mixed with butter until crisp.

Use as a cracker for the sardines.

Chintexle

Squash Seeds, Chile, Black Beans and Shrimp

1 cup (116 g) green
   squash seeds (pumpkin
   seeds can be
   substituted)
3 guajillo chiles
1 cup (253 g) cooked black
   beans
¼ cup (57 g) dried shrimp
Corn tortillas

Prepare the chiles as in the recipe for iguana. Toast the squash seeds and shrimp lightly in a *comal* or frying pan.

Mix all of these in a *molcajete* or blender, adding enough water or stock to make a thick paste.

Seviche Estilo Acapulco

Seviche, Acapulco Style

Chop fish into ½-inch (1½ cm) pieces, and marinate in lime juice. Overnight is best, but at least 3 or 4 hours until it turns white.

Remove fish from the lime juice.

Mix all of the ingredients together and refrigerate for an hour.

Serve with crackers on a bed of lettuce.

2 pounds (1 kg) white fish fillets
1½ cup (337 ml) lime juice
1 pound (450 g) tomatoes, chopped
2 small onions, chopped
⅔ cup (107 g) chopped olives
4 serrano or jalapeño chiles, fresh or canned, chopped
1 cup (167 ml) catsup
1 cup (225 ml) white wine
3 tablespoons (19 g) chopped cilantro
Salt
Pepper

Seviche con Leche de Coco

Seviche with Coconut Milk

3 pounds (1½ kg) white
   fish fillets
1½ cups (337 ml) lime
   juice
1 cup (182 g) grated
   coconut
Milk of 2 coconuts, about
2 cups (454 ml)
3 tomatoes, chopped
2 serrano chiles, chopped
1 teaspoon Tabasco
1 teaspoon pepper
Salt
2 tablespoons (8 g)
   chopped parsley
Avocado (optional)

Cut fish into ½-inch (1½ cm) pieces, and marinate in lime juice. Overnight is best.

Grate coconut meat until you have 1 cup. The coconut pieces can also be put in a blender. Add to coconut milk.

Remove fish from marinade, and mix all of the ingredients together. Refrigerate for an hour.

Serve with crackers on a bed of lettuce, with parsley and little scoops of avocado (if used) on top.

Pulpo a la Mexicana

Octopus Seviche with Beer

Heat oil in pan. Simmer tomatoes, chiles, and onion with salt and pepper for 5 minutes.

Add octopus, cilantro, and beer. Cover and simmer 5 minutes.

4 tomatoes, chopped
1 chile dulce (or ½ bell pepper), chopped
1 chile xcatic, chopped
1 small onion, chopped
Salt
Pepper
1 pound (½ kg) octopus, cut in pieces
1½ tablespoons (5 g) chopped cilantro
1 beer
2 tablespoons (28 ml) oil

Pulpo en su Tinta

Octopus in its Ink

Marinate octopus in lime juice ½ hour or more. Boil octopus in water with salt, bay leaf, and cumin until done, about 1½ hours. Peel skin off the octopus, if desired, and cut into bite-size pieces.

Peel and chop the roasted garlic. Fry with onion, bell pepper, and chile for 10 minutes.

Stir in vinegar, ink, wine, and tomato paste. Add 1 cup (227 ml) water and simmer until it thickens a little. Stir in octopus and serve. Salt if necessary.

2 pounds (1 kg) octopus, ink sack intact
Juice of 2 limes
Salt
1 bay leaf
½ teaspoon (1 g) ground cumin
5 cloves garlic, roasted
2 tablespoons (28 ml) oil
2 onions, chopped
½ bell pepper, chopped
1 chile xcatic, roasted and chopped
3 tablespoons (42 ml) vinegar
3 ounces (90 ml) red wine (optional)
3 ounces (85 g) tomato paste

Pulpo en Escabeche

Octopus in Vinegar

2 pounds (1 kg) octopus
Juice of 2 limes
2 bay leaves
5 onions, thinly sliced and
   cut across
½ bell pepper, chopped
1 chile xcatic
1 head garlic, roasted
½ teaspoon (2.5 g) allspice
3 tablespoons (43 ml) oil
⅓ cup (83 ml) vinegar
½ teaspoon (2.5 g) ground
   cumin
½ teaspoon (2.5 g)
oregano
½ teaspoon (2.5 g) pepper
Salt

Marinate octopus in lime juice for at least ½ hour.

Boil octopus in salted water with bay leaves until done, about 1½ hours. Peel skin off, if desired.

Fry onion, bell pepper, chile, garlic, and allspice in oil 5 to 7 minutes.

Add vinegar and octopus, and simmer 5 minutes. Add cumin and oregano and season to taste with salt and pepper. Cool and serve.

Pan de Cazón

Shark Bread – Minced Shark Tortilla Sandwich

Although pan de cazón is said to have originated in Campeche, it is a common afternoon botana all over the Yucatán. Some botanas that can accompany the pan de cazón are sliced beets and red onion marinated in lime, sliced cucumber marinated in lime, boiled and chopped potatoes with peas, sliced boiled carrots, and mayonnaise.

Boil the fish in salted water until done. Add 6 tomatoes and cook until they are done. Remove fish from water. Remove skin and shred. Squeeze.

Fry two chopped tomatoes and one chopped onion in oil with fish, salt, and pepper for 10 minutes.

Peel tomatoes that boiled with fish. Grind with a *molcajete*, or put in a blender.

Sauté the other onion until soft, and add peeled tomatoes.

Spread some refried beans on a tortilla and put it on a plate. Put some shark mixture over the refried beans. Put another tortilla on top.

Put tomato over it and serve. Garnish with roasted, chopped *habanero* chiles as desired.

2 pounds (1 kg) shark, cut in strips
Salt
8 tomatoes
2 onions, chopped
2 tablespoons (28 ml) oil
Pepper
Refried black beans
About 20 tortillas
2 *habanero* chiles, roasted and chopped

Langosta en Crema

Cream of Lobster

2 pounds (1 kg) lobster
1 cup (226 g) mayonnaise
6 ounces (177 ml) medium
    cream
Salt
Pepper

Boil lobster about 10 minutes. Remove the meat and blend or smash with a *molcajete*. Mix the other ingredients with the lobster.

Serve with tostadas or saltine crackers and avocado slices.

Alberto served Seviche Acapulco Style at his studio/restaurant near Acapulco. Thanks to the prickly pear cactus, *ensalada de nopalitos* can be enjoyed almost anywhere in Mexico.

These colorful garnishes of pickled onions, red salsa, and green salsa can accompany any repast from afternoon *botanas* to evening dinners.

Sopa de lima, a specialty of the Yucatán, nopal broth with shrimp and shrimp consommé, are delicious and nourishing elements of any meal.

Beef stuffed with ham and eggs floating in tomato sauce is an elegant and easy to prepare dish.

A rich preparation of pork stuffed with prunes called pork with cider is a complete meal, *muy sabroso*.

Sunday is *puchero* day in the Yucatán because it is easy to make in large quantities and there is a lot of house to house visiting on that day.

Potaje is another Sunday dish and depending on the size of the party both *puchero* and this dish are prepared.

Roast chicken in chile ancho is a simple sounding recipe that belies the care necessary in preparation. It is worth every minute.

Melt-in-the-mouth is the only way to describe chicken crêpes with chipotle chiles and walnuts. Be sure to prepare enough of them because they disappear.

Fish baked with achiote and wine and served on a banana leaf can convince guests that you are an aficionado.

You will discover that shrimp with tequila has quite an unusual flavor and it can be prepared in little time.

This beautiful cantaloupe tart is a scene stealer and a lovely finale to a Yucatecan dinner.

SALSAS

Salsas are what make food interesting and this is as true in the Yucatán as anywhere else. Salsas can influence the flavor of just about any dish. Some are traditionally served with specific foods. The salsas in this section are the ones that can be served with almost any food. Elsewhere in the book salsas will be with individual recipes.

Salsa de Tomate Sencillo

Simple Tomato Sauce

3 tomatoes, roasted,
  broiled, or boiled and
  coarsely mashed
½ onion, chopped
2 or 3 sprigs cilantro,
  pinched into pieces
3 or 4 small hot chiles
1 larger mild chile
Juice from a lime, or more
  to taste
2 tablespoons (28 ml)
  peanut or olive oil
Pinch of oregano
Salt
Sometimes ½ cucumber,
  peeled and diced

Mix the ingredients together, adjust seasonings to taste.

GREEN SALSA 1

6-8 tomatillos, husks
  removed
3 *serrano* chiles or other
  small, hot chiles
2 cloves garlic, peeled
2 or 3 sprigs cilantro,
  chopped
Salt

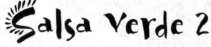

Salsa Verde 1

Green Salsa

Put tomatilllos and chiles in boiling water until soft. Mix all of the ingredients in a blender.

GREEN SALSA 2

½ pound (225 g) tomatillos
1-1½ cups (227-337 ml)
  water
2 cloves garlic
1 tablespoon (15 g)
  chopped cilantro
Salt

Salsa Verde 2

Green Salsa 2

Remove skins from tomatillos. Add water to cover and boil 5 minutes. Blend with other ingredients in a blender or with a *molcajete*. Very simple, *muy sabroso*.

Xni-Pec
Tomato and Chile Relish

Mix all ingredients together.

8-10 tomatoes, chopped
2 onions, chopped
2 *habanero* chiles (or to
    taste), chopped
Juice from 2 sour oranges
    (or lime, or a mixture of
    lime and orange juice)
Chopped cilantro to taste
Salt

Salsa Roja
Red Salsa

Prepare the tomatoes as in the recipe for iguana; prepare the chiles as for Budín Azteca. Mix all ingredients and grind with a *molcajete*, or coarsely in a blender.

4 tomatoes
1 onion, finely chopped
2 tablespoons (6.2 g)
    finely chopped cilantro
Salt

Guacamole con Tomatillos

Avocado and Tomatillo Sauce

3 *jalapeño* chiles
3 large or 4 small tomatillos
2 avocados
1 lime
1 medium onion, finely
  chopped
1 clove garlic, peeled
2 tablespoons (6.2 g)
  chopped cilantro leaves
Salt

Remove the seeds and veins from the chiles and chop finely.

Remove husks and boil the tomatillos in enough water to cover for 5 minutes.

Remove skin from avocados.

Squeeze the juice from the lime with the other ingredients, and mix in a blender or with a *molcajete*.

Hasikilpac

Squash Seed Dip

Mix all together. It should have the consistency of a standard dip for chips.

- 5 large boiled tomatoes
- 12 ounces (340 g) squash seeds, toasted and ground
- ½ cup (72 g) green part of green onions, finely chopped
- 2 teaspoons (2 g) chopped cilantro
- 1 *habanero* chile, chopped
- Small amount of water from boiled tomatoes, approximately ½ cup (114 ml)
- Salt

Recado Colorado

Achiote Paste

"Start from scratch" has more flavor than what is sold packaged in some markets.

Crush the annatto seeds in a *molcajete*. Mash all the ingredients together to make a paste. Wrap in plastic or foil. This will keep a long time.

- 2 tablespoons (30 g) annatto seeds
- 3 cloves garlic, peeled
- ½ teaspoon (.3 g) ground cumin
- Pinch of black pepper
- ½ teaspoon (.3 g) oregano
- A couple pinches ground allspice
- 2 tablespoons (28 ml) lime juice, or a combination of lime and vinegar

Salsa de Queso Oaxaqueña

Oaxacan Cheese Sauce

¾ pound (338 g) Oaxacan
cheese (another cheese
that is creamy when
melted can be
substituted)
1 pound (½ kg) tomatoes
1 bell pepper
1 *jalapeño* chile
5 cloves garlic, peeled
1 inch (2½ cm) of the
white part of a leek, or
small onion
1 nopal leaf (paddle)
1 cup (227 ml) strong
chicken stock
½ cup (114 g) butter
½ cup (114 g) flour

Prepare the cactus paddle as for "fish baked with nopals."

Coarsely chop all of the ingredients except the cheese and nopal, and simmer in the chicken stock about 10 minutes. Blend all but the cheese, and put in a pan to simmer.

Heat the butter in a separate pan, adding the flour while stirring until it is smooth. Gradually add the grated cheese, stirring until it is creamy. Add a little milk if necessary.

Stir the cheese mixture into the rest of the ingredients.

Good as a dip and on vegetables.

Crema de Aguacate

Avocado and Cream Dip

Blend.

Otilo uses this as a dip and to accompany fish and meat.

1 avocado
6 ounces (177 ml) medium
  cream
Salt
Pepper

Chutney de Coco y Cilantro

Coconut and Cilantro Chutney

Blend ingredients together coarsely.

½ cup (114 g) grated
  coconut
1 small onion, sliced
2 cloves garlic, peeled
2 pickled *jalapeños*
½ teaspoon (1 g) powdered
  ginger, or an equivalent
  amount of fresh ginger
¼ teaspoon (1 g) ground
  cumin
3 tablespoons (10 g)
  cilantro leaves
Juice of 2 limes
¼ teaspoon (1.5 g) sugar
1 teaspoon (6.2 g) salt

Mole Negro Oaxaqueño

Blackened Mole from Oaxaca

1 pound (450 g) chiles
   anchos
½ pound (225 g) chiles
   guajillos
½ pound (225 g) chiles
   pasillas mexicano (a
   black, dried chile)
1 *plátano macho* (frying
   banana, called *plátano*
   in the U.S.)
1 medium onion
1 head garlic
2 pounds (1 kg) tomatoes
¼ pound (113 g) raw
   peanuts (if unavailable,
   roasted peanuts with-
   out the skins will work)
¼ pound (113 g) pecans
¼ pound (113 g) sesame
   seeds
1 tablespoon (.6 g) dry
   crumbled oregano
4 cloves
¼ teaspoon (1.5 g)
   cinnamon
½ teaspoon (2.5 g) black
   pepper
2 hard-crusted rolls
Salt
Oil
2 2-pound (2 1-kg)
   chickens

Remove veins and seeds from the chiles. Save the seeds. Roast the chiles on a very hot, dry *comal* or frying pan, until they are crisp and black, 20 minutes to ½ hour. This can be done more quickly over an open flame. The room should be well ventilated because the smoke is very pungent. Sprinkling the chiles with rubbing alcohol helps. Roast the seeds until they are completely blackened ashes, about 10 minutes.

Peel the *plátano*, cut in ½-inch (1½ cm) strips, and put on a paper towel a few minutes to absorb some of the juice. Fry in ¼-inch (1 cm) oil about 2 minutes on each side; or you can fry slowly for up to ½ hour. The *plátano* gets sweeter as it cooks.

Roast the onion and garlic as in recipe for iguana, and blend with the tomatoes. Fry in oil for 10 minutes.

Toast the nuts and sesame seeds in a dry pan, but do not burn them like the chiles.

Grind the seeds, nuts, and spices together.

Add salt and blend everything, including *plátano* and rolls, together in a blender or with a *molcajete*. Add a little water, if necessary.

This recipe is sufficient for basting two chickens. Put the mixture in a pot, and add enough water to almost immerse chickens. Stir. Salt chickens, put in sauce, and simmer, covered until done, about an hour. Add a little water if needed. Uncover, if necessary, to thicken the sauce.

Kol

White Sauce

Melt the butter with a little chicken stock, and stir in the flour until the ingredients form a paste. Continue to add chicken stock, stirring until the mixture resembles a thick soup.

To serve, cut a wedge of stuffed cheese from recipe for Quesa Relleno and place in a bowl. Spoon a heaping portion of *kol* over the cheese. Spoon tomato sauce over the *kol*. Depending on the amount of *kol* used, the cheese and meat will be more or less "swimming" in it.

2 tablespoons (30 g) butter
1 cup (140 g) all-purpose
   flour or *masa*
Chicken stock
Salt to taste

MÉRIDA AND ITS ENVIRONS

For years I heard nothing but positive comments about Mérida: "It's like something out of a Humphrey Bogart movie—you'll love it," "It's one of my favorite cities in the world," "Mérida has soul." Indeed, Mérida is not just another city. Because of the weather, Mérida's buildings look old in a hurry, and when they are restored, they are restored as they were. Baking in the sun and soaking in the rain, they will soon be old again. Faded paint and pieces of plaster begin chipping off their walls, and mold starts creeping up from their bases. An auto parts store can seem as precious as an ancient Maya ruin.

Fronts of small shops open from wall to wall onto the sidewalks. Strolling around town, one can look inside and see people fabricating, repairing, and selling clothes, leather, or hardware. One can even watch coffins being made.

Mérida has grown dramatically over the last several years. Although signs at the entry to the city report a population of 563,000, it is believed to be nearly twice that amount. As industry moved to Mérida, job seekers did, too, flocking to the city from all parts of Mexico. As a result, a large percentage of today's populace is not native to the area. Nor does the city retain its former ambience as the capital of a Mexican colony. Instead, it is very much a working segment of Mexico.

I can no longer say that I have never heard anyone speak disparagingly of Mérida. Shortsighted critiques have come my way, primarily from tourists who had arrived at the bus station eager to evacuate on the next express. But I have also known people who came to town ten or fifteen years ago tell me that, although they used to like it, for it was a beautiful city, they no longer do. Had I not felt at home in Mérida in the early 1980s, I do not know how I would feel about it now.

Mérida Today

Mérida's narrow streets do not accommodate the ever-increasing traffic comfortably. Noise pollution is most offensive around the exquisite *zócalo* and the 400-year-old buildings surrounding it. In the early 1990s, concerned policymakers drafted a proposal to close these central streets to traffic permanently—a measure already instituted in Oaxaca—but store owners fought

29

it and won. Considering the large number of vehicles in Mérida, such an approach may not be practical, though something could be done about the noise they make. The clamor emitted by Carabella motorcycles, buses, and Volkswagen vans far exceeds the noise levels of their counterparts in other countries.

How the horse-drawn buggies manage to compete with the internal combustion engine seems to defy numerous laws of physics. Alas, pulling buggies in 100-degree weather and breathing the air that they do, these horses must have short lives. And they cannot put napkins in their ears as I do when sitting downtown in the daytime.

Even so, I cannot imagine a crowded, noisy city with more charm—more "soul"—than Mérida. Aside from the congestion on its streets, Mérida continues to look much like it used to. Its *Paseo Montejo* is often likened to the *Champs Élysées* in Paris. To me, Mérida's tree-lined boulevard is much more beautiful. Until recently, it was bordered on both sides by mansions. Many are still there. Some continue on as homes; others have been converted to offices; and still others have been replaced by more pragmatic enterprises. Tall, modern hotels have sprung up. In addition, a McDonald's and a supermarket have appeared where a large decaying mansion stood only five years ago. The changes have been accomplished tastefully, considering the difficulty of tearing down a once stately mansion and replacing it with such establishments tastefully.

Mérida also has its generic outskirts—fast-food chains, high office buildings, and shopping malls. Yet, even these are interspersed among small businesses that would look out of place in most modern cities.

With the influx of people from other parts of Mexico has come a variety of foods. Many sidewalk cafés that open at night along *Paseo Montejo* do not serve traditional Yucatecan fare. Instead, they offer *tacos al pastor, quesadillas de cuitlacoche,* and *frijoles charros,* all from central Mexico.

Some older restaurants in the center of town now offer pizza and hamburgers along with their daily specials of *frijol con puerco* (pork with black beans) (p. 121) or *pavo en relleno negro* (blackened stuffed turkey) (p. 161) or other regional favorites. In the center of town as well as on its outskirts, the easiest food to find at night is hotdogs. The ubiquitous hotdog is available from street vendors who operate mobile carts, the most elaborate of which are also stocked with *hamburguesas.*

Dishes native to the Yucatán remain unchanged by this inpouring of ethnically diverse foods. In Mérida, culinary styles from many parts of the world remain intact, peacefully coexisting side by side.

Another facet of life in the working city of Mérida is that its residents like to evacuate at certain times of the year for a change of pace. Progreso is the main beach town for Merídians. Radiating eastward and westward from Progreso are *puertos* (small towns) dotted by houses that range from large expensive houses to concrete-block boxes.

Every July and August people from Mérida invade these coastal towns like troops, as though Dwight D. Eisenhower were directing them. This two-month phenomenon is called *la temporada* (the season). A similar deluge occurs for a shorter period of time during *semana santa* (Easter week). In preparation for both these events, house rentals triple, even quadruple, and Merídians take up occupancy by the hundreds. The rest of the year these locales are virtual ghost towns, even though their air and water temperatures remain warm.

During *la temporada,* established restaurants as well as shacks with *"pescado frito por kilo"* painted on a wall sell fried *mero* (grouper) and other fish by the kilo. The air is so permeated with the aroma of fresh fish frying that it is hard to be there without stopping for one.

A sometime diversion for Merídians is a party that is held in the city the first Friday of every month. These gatherings were originally hosted by the American Embassy but are now privately sponsored in bars or restaurants. Many of the people at these parties are "snowbirds" from the United States and Canada, *norteamericanos* on business in Mérida and expatriots living in "Gringo Gulch."

While not an officially designated district, Gringo Gulch encompasses about ten square blocks near the center of Mérida. A number of United States citizens own homes here, although some are inhabited only part-time. The residents of Gringo Gulch tend to seek the companionship of other gringos and, as a rule, have little desire to learn much Spanish. Here, housing is inexpensive and English is the primary language.

While talking with a Gringo Gulch homeowner at a Friday party just after I had arrived in Mérida in 1994, I told her I had decided to move to the beach for a few weeks before the prices went up.

"If you go to the beach, don't go to Chelem," she said. "People who wind up there are those who have hit absolute rock bottom, those who can't go any lower."

When I told her I was planning to rent a house on the beach in Chelem the following week, she laughed and said, "You're an exception."

I told her that was the nicest thing anyone had said to me the entire day.

"Houses fore Rent"

A hand-painted sign was taped to a post in front of a house near the beach in Chelem. The English portion of the sign read, "Houses fore Rent"; the Spanish part was spelled correctly. I knocked on the door.

The lady of the house answered and introduced herself as Petra. She told me she rents and sells houses in the greater Chelem area. After informing her that I was looking for a house on the beach until the start of *la temporada,* she took me to see some homes.

I rented the house across the sandy dirt street from Petra, her husband Bill, and their children—twenty-two-year-old Margarita and seventeen-year-old Carlos. It was a spacious home with the Gulf of Mexico for a front yard. A permanent front-yard feature was the red dinghy which turned out to be Bill's boat. I had a beautiful view and was only fifty yards from the water. At that distance, the plastic bottles and wrappers on the beach were invisible.

"Come over when you finish unloading," Bill said, as I signed the rental papers. So just as the sun was about to set, I paid him a visit.

While Bill and I sat on the patio in front of his house, many people passed by. He greeted them all. They acknowledged him with a nod and a "Guillermo." Every now and then I could hear passersby whispering to one another as they approached. "Guillermo, he likes fishing," they would say, a Mona Lisa smile on their faces.

As Bill and I talked, I learned that he and Petra had been married twenty-three years. Petra was from a poor family in Puerto Angel, Oaxaca. Bill, twenty-five years her senior, was from Virginia. He had served in the marines and been hit three times while in Korea, so with an early retirement pension he bought a Triumph motorcycle and went journeying through Mexico. One of his stops was Puerto Angel.

After a while, Petra came out to join us. She talked a little about her life in Oaxaca. Her family had lived in a meager dirt-floor house by the Pacific Ocean. Her seven brothers were fishermen. All they had to eat, other than on special occasions, were beans, tortillas, lobster, shrimp, and fish. All they were able to hear were each other's voices and the ocean.

Petra's English was not much better than Bill's Spanish, but then, she had never lived in an English-speaking country. Aggravated by Bill's inability to speak Spanish, she said, "Twenty-four years he live, and he no know nothing!" She emphasized the *nothing* with her hands the same way an umpire signals "Safe!" on a close call.

"Hell," said Bill, "at my age what's the use of learning a new language? I wouldn't be around long enough to speak it." At that, his wife went into the house.

Petra had a problem pronouncing my name, as many Mexicans do. She called me "Lime." Bill could pronounce my name with no trouble, but he had to think before saying it. He usually called me "uh Lyman."

"That's right about her family, uh Lyman," Bill continued. "They didn't have anything. She's never been to school. I used to sit in a hammock with her and try to teach her simple math. But I didn't teach her much—I guess I didn't have the patience for it. Now she can read and write and do arithmetic as good as I can. I don't know how she learned."

Just as the sun dipped below the horizon, Bill launched into a fishing story. "I spent three nights out there in a boat smaller than that one," he said, pointing to the nine-foot dinghy in my new front yard. "The anchor rope broke, and the motor wouldn't start. I put the sail up, but it was rotten and kept tearing. I spent three nights out there with a quart of water and nothing to eat but my bait and a couple of little fish I had caught. I don't even like fish. I burned up in the day and froze at night. I was twenty miles out when they found me. They said I was missing on the radio and in the Progreso paper. Everybody probably thought I was dead. The house was full of people when I got home. I don't know if they were mourning or celebrating."

He went on to say that twice he had to swim back after his boat had turned over. The first time, he swam for five hours. The second, he said, was easy—he returned in only an hour and a half.

"The second word on that sign is misspelled," I told him, hoping to divert him from his tragedies at sea.

"I noticed that the other day, uh Lyman. I meant to bring it up," he explained. Then he called, "Mama!" Petra came out. "The sign's not spelled right. 'Fore' has too many letters in it."

I got up, walked over to the sign, and covered the "e."

"*¿Si?*" she asked. Then she called, "*¡Margarita!*" When her daughter appeared, Petra pointed the problem out to her. They discussed how to fix the lettering. Margarita, evidently, was the artistic one in the family.

Bill was proud to be putting his daughter through college. "She goes to school in Mérida," he told me. "She wants to teach something called special education."

When I got up to leave, Bill said: "We'll have to go fishing in a couple of days—maybe next week. First I've got to get my motor fixed. I don't know what's wrong with it, but I'm going to take it to the repair shop tomorrow." Then he paused. "You probably don't want to go with me after what I told you," he added with a smile that almost broke into a laugh. Bill does not laugh much, but he smiles a lot.

"I'd like to go fishing," I told him.

In the morning Petra brought me a plate of *huevos revueltos con chaya* (scrambled eggs with *chaya* (page 65) and some leftover *makum de pescado* (a fish dish) (page 175). *Chaya,* a green leafy vegetable, is similar in appearance to spinach but provides more protein carbohydrates, calcium, iron, phosphorus, niacin, and vitamins A, B-1, B-2, and C. Although not commonly served in restaurants, it is prepared in the home kitchen in a variety of ways: boiled and chopped *chaya* is mixed with *masa* balls to be simmered with beans, or *chaya* is cooked with rice or potatoes, and sometimes it is fried with pork chops.

After handing me this surprise breakfast, Petra mentioned that a neighbor had just given her several fish between twelve and eighteen inches long. She would be salting and drying them that afternoon, and I was welcome to watch her do it.

When I arrived later in the day, Petra was in her backyard already at work on the fish. The best ones for salting and drying, she said, are those with white meat, such as shark, white bonito, tuna, sailfish, marlin, rays, sea bass, and grouper. *Huachinango* (red snapper), however, will not work well because its meat is too fine.

Talking as she worked, Petra cut through the back of a fish so it could be opened out flat. Next she removed the intestines, backbone, and gills but left the scales and the skin. After cutting slits across the meat on the insides of the fish, she packed the slits with salt, then rubbed the rest of the fish with more salt. Finally, she exposed the insides of the fish to the sun by draping its body over the clothesline. After a full day of drying, the salted fish are swirled in water, she explained. Some people dip them in the ocean because they believe that keeps flies away during the next stage of drying. The fish are then returned to the clothesline for another four or five days, during which time their position is changed so that all parts of them receive equal sunlight. One must remember, however, to bring the fish in at night, she said with something approaching embarrassment—not only to protect them from nocturnal predators but to keep them out of the moonlight. If the moon is in a certain place in the sky, she warned, the fish exposed to it will turn mushy.

The procedure for salting and drying large fish, such as shark and marlin, is slightly different, Petra continued. First one must fillet them, skin them, and salt both sides of the meat. If they are thick, they may be slit and salted, as with whole fish. Then both sides must be exposed equally to the sun. Dried fish, whether whole or filleted, will last four or five months unrefrigerated, she added.

When all Petra's fish had been draped over the clothesline and the sticks, she went inside and wrote out dried fish recipes for me to try. Included were directions for making *pescado seco salado* (dried salted fish) (p. 187) and *filete de pescado seco salado* (dried salted fish fillet) (p. 188), as well as *salsa de chile ancho* (p. 189), an alternate sauce for the fillets.

Petra was full of culinary surprises. One Monday morning she brought me a serving of *frijol con puerco* (pork with black beans) (page 121) with *salsa de tomate sencilla* (simple tomato salsa, p. 20). This Yucatecan dish, she said, is typically served on Mondays, because after the weekend people are *flojos* (idlers, slowpokes) and want to prepare easy meals. Sitting on a little bench by my front yard, she proceeded to describe other dishes she cooks when she feels like a *flojo*. She told me how to make *puerco entomatado* (pork stew in tomato sauce) (p. 120) and *carne de res recado colorado* (beef pot roast with achiote (p. 99).

She also gave me recipes for cooking Oaxacan recipes such as iguana.

A few days later, Progreso's first chain supermarket opened its doors to the public. Petra braved the crowds that had been drawn there by the novelty as well as the savings and bought a lot of the week's *oferta* (special offer). That week she brought me three pork dishes: *costillas de puerco a la parrilla* (grilled pork ribs) (p. 119), *tiras de puerco con cola* (pork strips in cola) (p.118), and *lomo de puerco al horno con cerveza* (pork loin baked with beer) (p.118).

One evening, organ music filled the air with tones loud enough to render a personal sound system useless. It sounded like the musical score for a class B horror movie. I looked out the window and, for the first time, saw lights on in the house next door to Bill and Petra's. Linda, possibly the only gringa in Chelem, was sitting on the bench by my house, watching the water—and, by necessity, listening to the music. She was housesitting and we had met briefly. I went out to chat with her.

"Who died?" she asked.

We discussed the music and decided it sounded more like a church funeral than a roller rink, the only two places we associated with organ music.

The following day I saw a woman and a boy sitting with Bill and Petra on their patio. I went over to say hello. The newcomers—Irma and her twenty-year-old son Alejandro—had just arrived from Mérida, their home. And yes, Irma had been responsible for the organ music. Her hands accompanied her voice as if she were still playing the organ. When the conversation comes around to food and cooking, as it always does with Irma, she uses her hands to do the cutting, adding of ingredients, mixing, and turning

After a while, Irma got up and started walking home. Halfway there she turned to make sure that her son was trailing after her."There's something wrong with that boy," Bill said. "I don't know what, but something's missing."

The bench outside my house was a popular late afternoon spot. It was in the shade. People would sit there in the evenings, too. Early one evening I joined Petra, Irma, and Blanca, another neighbor. They had been discussing *la temporada,* which was only two weeks away. Petra said that by this time the previous year, the upstairs apartment in their house had been rented, but now the economy was so bad that they might not have tenants at all. Usually, they rented their house and stayed at the house of a Floridian who returned to Miama during *la temporada.* She went on to complain about her husband, stating, "He keeps saying he is going to paint the front of the house, but *no hace nada!*" She emphasized the *nada* (nothing) by stomping her foot.

Blanca had a stall at the market in Chelem. She said that she sold crab there, and business would soon be picking up. Irma corrected her emphatically, shaking her head and wagging her index finger back and forth like a windshield wiper—Mexican sign language for "No way." Irma reminded her that she sold vegetables, and her sister sold crab.

"*Si,*" Blanca said, somewhat dejectedly, her momentary surge in status gone. I commented that I had never seen *jaibas rellenas* (deviled crab) in Mexico.

"We have it here," Blanca said. "You don't see it in restaurants, but people make it at home."

The three of them then told me how they make *jaibas rellenas*. Petra mixes ground pork with the crabmeat *(jaiba rellena con chilmole)* (p. 198). Blanca stuffs the shells with a crab and fish mixture *(chilpachole de jaibas)* (p. 199). Irma stuffs the shells with a similar mixture but adds three chopped tomatoes to it and more white wine than vinegar. In lieu of a sauce, she puts *bread crumbs* and a little *butter* on top of the stuffed shells and bakes them until golden. Irma is from Mérida, and Blanca is from Chelem.

Blanca had grown up looking at animal innards as they hung like pendulums in the market in Chelem. She worked in the market where various foods are sold near each other. Unexposed to supermarket packaging, which tends to disguise what most meat was originally designed to do, she uses an assortment of meats in her cooking. Insisting that I sample some, she brought me some *hígado de res con recado colorado* (beef liver with achiote) (p. 104) one night. Other times she stopped by with *riñón de res con Jerez* (beef kidney with sherry) (p. 105), *pezuñas con garbanzos* (pigs feet with garbanzos) (p. 122), *sopa de ostión* (oyster soup) (p. 50), or *mondongo andaluza* (tripe soup with garbanzos) (p. 60), southern Mexico's counterpart to the *menudo* of the north.

About a month before the start of *la temporada,* a Dutch woman came looking for a place to rent. Her adopted daughter, a native of Colombia, was holding a fish. She had caught it using a hook and piece of line she had found on the sand, along with a scrap of bread for bait. Bill was so astounded by this success that he talked about it for days. He was sure the child was charmed.

Petra rented them a house down the beach for a month. As they prepared to drive off and unpack, Bill said he would take the two of them fishing in a few days. Soon afterward he extended the same invitation to an American couple who rented the upstairs apartment for three days. Neither twosome went fishing during their stay in Chelem.

Hell, I Go Fishing

My six-week sojourn in Chelem went by quickly. The Saturday morning of my last weekend in town, I heard loud talking from across the street. Looking out the window, I noticed two men I had not seen before walking away from Bill and Petra's house. I also noticed a fresh coat of paint on the lower half of their house. Half wondering what was going on, I walked over to commend Bill on the paint job.

"Have a seat, uh Lyman," Bill offered, his shoulder twitching. The most severe of his three hits in Korea had been to his shoulder and had caused nerve damage. As a result, when he was excited, his shoulder twitched. His friends had left him with a bottle of brandy.

"I see you've painted the house," I said.

"Yeah, I still have the top to do. My body doesn't take it like it used to. I stopped to rest a while, then Pops and Big John came over with a jug. Now it's so hot that I'll have to finish painting in the morning. We've got to get it ready; someone will come along to rent it.

Petra walked up and looked at the paint job. *"¡Que pasó?"* she asked.

"I'll finish in the morning, Mama. It's too damn hot."

She walked into the house pressing her fingertips against an imaginary head the size of a beach ball.

"She says I don't do nothing," Bill muttered, looking at me. "Hell, I go fishing."

At that moment, we saw Irma and Alejandro walking up. "Would you mind moving that paint bucket, uh Lyman?" Bill asked. "The boy's sure to step in it. I call him Mr. Magoo, but I shouldn't make fun of him; I feel sorry for him.

While hauling the bucket around to the side of the house, I could hear Bill calling out, with his unusual accent, *"Buenos días, Irma."* Then he hollered, *"¡Petra, Irma está aquí!"*

The five of us sat outside and chatted. After a brief discussion about the heat, the subject turned to food. Irma said she was going to make *pollo en adobo blanco a la naranja* (chicken in spices with orange juice) (p. 155) later in the day. She performed hand gestures to demonstrate its preparation, then kissed her fingertips and invited me to dinner. She goes to a lot of trouble to cook good food, she explained, but her family won't eat it.

"She cooks enough for an army," Bill interjected, "and she ends up giving it to the dog."

Irma talked constantly while preparing the chicken. At last it was ready and was served with rice and avocado. Alejandro picked at his chicken and ate mostly Bimbo bread, a Mexican brand name similar to Wonder bread with butter. I could understand her frustration, cooking each night for herself and the dogs.

While eating, Irma talked about what she was going to prepare for dinner the next day. Sunday—when families gather together—is *puchero* day in the Yucatán, she said, because the stew is easy to make in large quantities. And it can accommodate a lot of food one wants to get rid of at the end of the week. Although *puchero* can be made with one type of meat, she explained, *puchero con tres carnes* (chicken, pork, and beef stew) (p. 124) is better. Irma went on to point out that, depending on the available ingredients, she sometimes makes *potaje* (pork, ham, and sausage stew) (p. 123) on Sundays instead.

On my last night in Chelem, Petra brought me some *pescado con chile ancho y jugo de naranja* (fish with *ancho* chile and orange juice) (p. 170) . "Maybe you come back in September, Lime, when houses no cost so much," she said.

The next morning while I was loading up my truck, Bill stopped by and said: "Come back and see us. Petra likes you, I like you, even Irma likes you. You're welcome any time." As I began to drive away, he hollered, "We'll have to go fishing in September, uh Lyman."

Independence Day in Gringo Gulch

It has been suggested that a large percentage of *norteamericanos* living full- or part-time in Mérida have been rejected by their native country. Certainly, many of them lead lives that deviate from the norms generally accepted in mainstream society. Most of those living in the greater Gringo Gulch area are retired, and some are quite wealthy. They attend numerous small get-togethers in which a major topic of conversation is people who are not present. In organizing such a party, one must be careful to exclude from the guest list anyone who is not liked by those who are on it

Everybody seems to like Alberto Castillo, and virtually all the residents of Gringo Gulch have at least one of his paintings hanging in their house. Because I am a friend of Alberto's, I was invited to a party in Gringo Gulch on the 16th of September to celebrate Mexico's independence from Spain, which took place in 1821.

The party was hosted by a man from the United States and his much younger Mexican wife. I had heard from a resident of the community that she had married him to get out of her parents' house. (It is not acceptable for a young Mexican woman to live alone.) I had heard from someone else that he came to Mexico to marry a young woman, and that twelve years later he still wished she were a young woman. Such are the things people in Gringo Gulch say.

I was wandering around trying to figure out where the party was when I came upon a Mexican resident of the neighborhood. I asked where Joe and Susana lived. He did not know. Then I mentioned that they were a married couple. "Oh," he replied, "the married couple," and he pointed to a house. Stepping inside, I realized that although the exteriors of the houses in the area were old and generic-looking, the interiors were lovely. This one, at least, certainly was.

The people at the party were a mix of El Salvadoran, Mexicans, *norteamericanos,* married couples, unmarried couples, single men of all ages, and single women over the age of about sixty; young women do not usually go to social events unaccompanied. A pretty Mexican girl was sitting in a corner by herself. Her eyes were red from crying. A young man sitting not far from her was playing a guitar softly to a couple nearby.

I was told to help myself to what turned out to be the most impressive potluck I had ever seen. These people were not trying to get by with potato chips or a pot of beans; they had brought culinary masterpieces. The girl who had been crying came to the table and began picking at several platters. When I commented on the pretty red, white, and green dish, she told me it was *chiles en nogada* (chiles with walnut sauce) (p. 103). The colors are those of the Mexican flag, she said, and the dish is traditional Independence Day fare from Puebla. Other specialties included *calabasas rellenas* (squash filled with ground pork) (p. 78), Alberto's *croquetas de pescado* (fish croquettes) (p. 9), *caserola de pescado y camarones con crema* (fish and shrimp casserole with cream) (p. 180), *frijoles charros* (ranch style beans) (p. 77), and *chicharrón con chile ancho* (cracklings with chile *ancho*) (p. 128).

I helped myself to small portions of all these dishes and sat down with a full plate. The sad girl sat beside me. Right away she began complaining about her El Salvadoran boyfriend—the one playing the guitar. She did not think he liked her anymore because he paid no attention to her.

"See," she said, "he doesn't care if I'm sitting next to him or not. I don't think he even knows. I'm going to leave him. It's been like this for more than a year. He wasn't this way when I met him. I don't know you, but I feel I can talk to you and tell you these things."

What she meant was that she had found someone new to tell them to. A guest at the party later disclosed that this was her customary form of conversation. They eventually took themselves and their problems to Canada.

After a while, I went back for more of Alberto's *croquetas de pescado,* but they were gone. "Yes, I ate them," he said, then joked, " I don't usually like my own cooking." I spent the rest of my time at the party tracing the other dishes to their makers and asking for recipes.

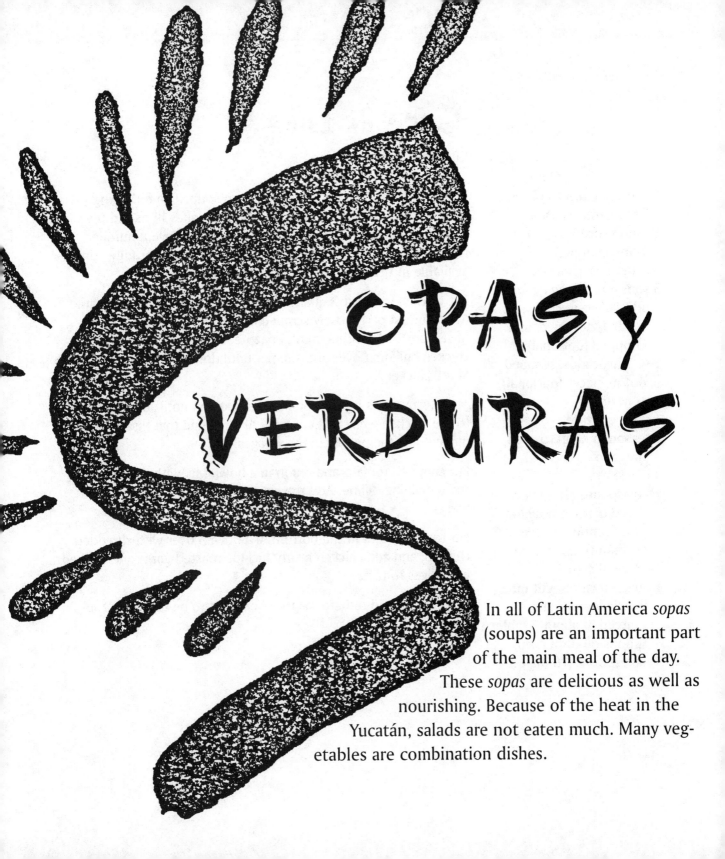

SOPAS Y VERDURAS

In all of Latin America *sopas* (soups) are an important part of the main meal of the day. These *sopas* are delicious as well as nourishing. Because of the heat in the Yucatán, salads are not eaten much. Many vegetables are combination dishes.

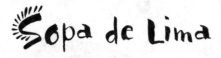Sopa de Lima

Chicken Soup with Lime

1 chicken cut into pieces
1 head garlic, roasted
½ onion sliced
1 onion chopped
4 tomatoes, chopped
3 sour limes (*lima agria*)
1 or 2 *habanero* chiles, seeded, deveined, and chopped (optional)
1 or 2 avocados, scooped out in pieces (optional)
1 stem mint
1 stem epazote
1 teaspoon (.6 g) toasted oregano
3 bay leaves
1½ teaspoons (10 g) powdered chicken bouillon (it is common in the Yucatán to use this in place of salt)
1 dozen tortillas (cut into ½-inch squares and sautéed in about 5 tablespoons oil until crisp)
5 tablespoons (70 ml) oil

This is a traditional Yucatecan chicken soup. The following recipe is how my friend Alberto Castillo makes it, as did his mother. Sour limes, available in the Yucatán, have a unique taste that is nothing like the more common sour orange. Limes available in the United States can be substituted.

Put chicken in about 2 quarts (2 l) water. Add sliced onion, garlic (with burned part loosely scraped off), 1 thinly sliced lime and juice from ½ of another, mint, epazote, bay leaves, oregano, and chicken buillon. Cover and simmer until done, about 40 minutes. Shred chicken.

Most restaurants fry the tomatoes and onion until soft and add it to the chicken while it is cooking. Alberto said that his mother made it like the people in the villages.

Put chopped tomato and onion in a bowl. Mix with the juice of the remaining ½ lime. Add the chopped *habanero* and avocado pieces.

Put tortilla pieces in the bottom of a bowl. Cover with shredded chicken, and add chicken broth. Include roasted garlic and cooked lime slices to taste.

Serve onion and tomato mixture in a bowl to be used as a topping.

Sopa de Aguacate

Avocado Soup

Cut avocado in half and scoop out the meat. Blend all the ingredients until smooth.

Chill and serve.

2 large avocados
1 medium onion
1 quart (1 l) half-and-half
½ teaspoon (2.5 ml)
   Tabasco
Salt
Pepper

Sopa de Aguacate con Crema

Cream of Avocado Soup

Blend avocado with chicken stock, chile powder, powdered bouillon, and cilantro.

Heat in a double boiler 10 minutes. This process of steaming food in the Yucatán is called a *baño de María*.

Allow to cool. Stir in cream, and chill.

1 large avocado
1 pint (¼ l) chicken stock
1 teaspoon (2.3 g) chile powder, or *al gusto*
1 tablespoon (3.3 g)
   powdered chicken
   bouillon
2 tablespoons (6.2 g)
   chopped cilantro
1 cup (225 ml) cream or
   half-and-half

Sopa de Flor de Calabaza

Squash Blossom Soup

15 squash blossoms
Pepper
Butter
1 onion, chopped
1 clove garlic, smashed
Powdered chicken
    bouillon
1 egg, beaten

Cut blossoms from stems and chop.

Fry them in butter with onion, garlic, and pepper for 2 or 3 minutes. Do not brown.

Add to a liter of water. Add chicken bouillon and bring to a boil. Slowly pour in beaten egg.

Cover and remove from heat.

Sopa de Calabacitas

Tender Squash Soup

2 pounds (1 kg) tender
    squash, chopped
1 large onion, finely
    chopped
3 cloves garlic, minced
2 tablespoons (6.2 g)
    minced cilantro
¼ pound (113 g) queso
    fresco or feta cheese
2 tablespoons (28 ml) oil
2 quarts (2 l) water
Salt

Fry the squash, onion, and garlic until soft, about 5 minutes. Add this and the cilantro to 2 quarts of salted boiling water. Simmer uncovered for 20 minutes. Sprinkle the crumbled cheese on top and serve.

 Sopa de Guias

Summer Squash Soup

Boil everything but *masa* and flowers for 20 minutes. Keep covered, if necessary, to keep water boiling. Add squash flowers and boil 10 minutes more. If using *masa*, melt butter and add to *masa*, along with salt and enough water to make balls about ¾ inch (2 cm) in diameter. Poke a finger into the ball, making little cups. Add for the last 10 minutes, along with the flowers. Some cooks do not use *masa* flour in *sopa de guias*.

3 feet (90 cm) of squash vines, tender ends are best

1 pound (½ kg) of small, tender calabazas (If they are not available, any other summer squash, such as yellow or zucchini can substitute. The squash used in Mexico are dark green, round like a wheel, and somewhat flat.)

1 onion, chopped

4 cloves garlic, minced

3 ears of corn, cut into 2-inch (4 cm) pieces

2 sprigs of parsley, chopped

3 tablespoons (9 g) *chepiles* (Can be omitted because neither I, nor anyone I know, knows what it is. It is used extensively in Oaxaca.)

3½ quarts (3 l) water

10-15 squash flowers

¼ pound (35 g) *masa* flour (optional)

1 tablespoon (15 g) butter (optional)

Salt

Crema de Calabaza Alberto

Cream of Zucchini Soup Alberto

8 zucchini, chopped
Salt
1 medium onion, chopped
(leek can be used
instead of onion)
1 tablespoon (14 ml) oil
1 chicken bouillon cube
1 quart (1 l) extra rich
milk (or a blend of milk
and cream)

Boil chopped zucchini 20 minutes in salted water. Drain and let cool. Sauté chopped onion in the oil only until soft. Dissolve bouillon cube in ½ cup (112 ml) water over burner. Put the vegetables, chicken stock, and milk in a blender. Heat, and it is ready to serve.

The same recipe can be used for carrots, broccoli, and most other vegetables.

Consommé de Camarón

Shrimp Consommé

2 medium shrimp, whole
¼ *serrano* chile, seeded,
deveined, and chopped
¼ teaspoon (1.5 g)
chopped epazote leaves
1 tablespoon (15 g)
chopped tomato
¼ teaspoon (1 g) catsup
Dash Worcestershire sauce
½ teaspoon (5 ml) oil
Salt

The consommé was served in a 6-ounce drinking glass. The following is for each 6-ounce serving.

Fry chopped tomato in oil for 5 minutes.

Put everything together, cover, and boil gently for 20 minutes.

Serve with lime wedges on the side.

Caldillo de Nopales

Nopal Broth

Boil *ancho* chiles 10 minutes, and grind in a *molcajete* with cloves, pepper, and cumin. Strain this mixture.

Fry the tomatoes, onion, and garlic in oil for 10 minutes.

Add everything except eggs to boiling water. Cover and simmer 25 minutes, making sure nopals are tender and *don't* squeak when chewed.

Beat eggs and stir into soup.

2 *ancho* chiles
2 cloves
5 peppercorns, or ¼ teaspoon black pepper
¼ teaspoon (.5 g) ground cumin
5 tomatoes, chopped
1 onion, chopped
4 cloves garlic, minced
2 tablespoons (30 ml) oil
4 nopal leaves, spines removed, and coarsely chopped in about ½-inch (1½ cm) pieces
¾ pound (340 g) shrimp
2 cups (508 g) *habas* (broad beans) or large lima beans, cooked
1 15-ounce (45-g) can peas (or its equivalent), drained
2 *jalapeño* chiles
2 sprigs epazote
2 quarts (2 l) water
Salt
2 eggs

Sopa de Ostión

Oyster Soup

Oil
3 tomatoes, chopped
1 small onion, chopped
½ bell pepper, chopped
1 clove garlic, minced
2 tablespoons (28 ml)
  vinegar
40 oysters and their juice
Salt
3 sprigs parsley, chopped

Fry tomatoes, onion, bell pepper, and garlic for 15 minutes until tender.

Add to 1 quart (1 l) water with vinegar, and bring to a boil. Add the oysters and turn the heat off.

Although not common in the Yucatán, I would say to add Worcestershire sauce *al gusto*. Serve garnished with chopped parsley.

Sopa de Ostión con Chile Ancho

Oyster Soup with Chile Ancho

Seed chiles, roast, and bring them to a boil in enough water to cover. Remove from heat and let cool. Blend with the tomatoes, garlic, and onion.

Fry everything in oil 10 minutes. Add salt to taste.

Bring 1½ quarts (1½ l) water to boil.

Add the chile mixture and the juice from the oysters, and simmer for 15 minutes. Add water if it is thicker than you want it to be.

Add oysters and continue to simmer until their edges begin to curl.

3 *ancho* chiles
3 tomatoes
2 cloves garlic
1 onion
2 tablespoons (28 ml) oil
Salt
1 pint (280 g) oysters

Caldo de Jaiba Isla Mujeres

Crab Soup from Isla Mujeres

17 Italian plum tomatoes
¼ onion
3 cloves garlic
5-7 canned *chipotle* chiles
   with some juice (or *al*
   gusto)
1 tablespoon (15 grams)
   powdered chicken
   bouillon
2 sprigs epazote
5 carrots, peeled and
   sliced thin
2 potatoes, chopped
   coarsely
1 pound (450 g) crab meat
2 tablespoons (28 ml) oil

Boil tomatoes about 5 minutes. Drain, reserving some of the liquid.

Sauté onion, garlic, and chiles in oil. Blend with tomatoes and their liquid.

Simmer with a little water from the boiled tomatoes until it cooks down, 20 to 30 minutes.

Bring 3 quarts (2¼ l) water with bouillon and epazote to a boil.

Add tomato mixture and let boil.

Add carrots and potatoes, and let boil about 20 minutes.

Add crab during last 10 minutes.

Sopa de Jaibas con Chilpachole

Crab Soup with Chile Ancho

Prepare chiles as in oyster soup with chiles *ancho*. Blend garlic, onions, and chiles in a little water from the chiles, or grind in the *molcajete*, chiles first.

Boil fish head with epazote in 2 quarts (2 l) or more salted water for 20 minutes.

Add all other ingredients and simmer for 10 minutes.

7 ancho chiles
3 cloves garlic
2 onions
1 fish head, or other pieces
1 sprig epazote
Salt
1 tablespoon (15 g) Maggi sauce
¾ pound (345 g) crab meat

Sopa de Calamar

Squid Soup

Fry garlic and onion in oil for 5 minutes.

Add wine and simmer slowly for 30 minutes.

Add vinegar, oregano, tomatoes, water, and squid. Simmer 15 minutes.

Add milks and chicken broth, heat, season to taste, and serve.

6 cloves garlic, minced
1 onion, chopped
2 tablespoons (28 ml) oil
1 cup (225 ml) white wine
1 tablespoon (14 ml) vinegar
1 teaspoon (.6 g) oregano
18 ounces (225 g) tomatoes, chopped
1 cup (225 ml) water
4 pounds (1800 g) squid, cleaned, cut into rings, and tentacles cut off
1 can evaporated milk
2 cups (450 ml) half-and-half
1 cup (225 ml) chicken broth
Salt

Sopa Campechana

Fish Soup from Campeche

1 2-pound (1-k) fish, cut
   diagonally into 6 pieces
Juice of 2 limes
Salt
Pepper
2 tablespoons (28 ml) oil
2 onions, sliced thin
4 tomatoes, sliced
3 tablespoons (24 g) *masa*
   flour or cornflower
Small can of *chipotle* chiles
1 sprig epazote

Marinate fish in lime for a few minutes with salt and pepper.

Fry onions in oil until soft. Add the tomatoes, salt, and pepper. Cover and let simmer a few minutes.

Add 6 cups (1350 ml) water. When it begins to boil, add fish.

Dissolve the flour in a little water. Add little by little, stirring.

Add the chiles and epazote.

Simmer 10 minutes.

Consommé de Pescado Isla Mujeres

Fish Consommé from Isla Mujeres

2 pounds (1 kg) fish heads,
   gills removed
3 tablespoons (42 ml)
   olive oil
2-3 heads garlic, roasted
   and peeled
5 bay leaves
8 peppercorns, ground
5 balls allspice, ground
4 cloves, ground
7 leaves oregano
1-2 *habanero* chiles (or *al
   gusto*)
Salt

This is a poor person's aphrodisiac and a cure all for any temporary minor illness.

Add all ingredients to 3½ quarts (3½ k) boiling water, and boil 45 minutes or until you choose to stop.

 Che chak

Simple Fish Soup

Otilio said that *che is* Maya for "rain stick", and *chak* is "rain". It is a very simple fish soup.

Cover fish fillets with water. Add oregano, garlic, lime, salt, and pepper. Boil about 2 minutes for ½-inch (1½ cm) thick fillets.

 Sopa de Pescado

Fish Soup

To make a broth with fish scraps and salted water, simmer the scraps for 40 minutes.

Prepare garlic, tomatoes, onion, as for iguana sauce. Put *jalapeño* in the pan to roast with the tomatoes. Knock or scrape the crisp ashes off. Grind with a *molcajete*, or chop coarsely with a blender. Fry in 1 tablespoon (14 ml) oil for about 10 minutes. Add to broth, along with fillets cut into chunks. Add a sprig of epazote if you have it, but it's not necessary. Cover and simmer 15 minutes. If there are any ashes they float on top. It looks nicer if these are skimmed off.

1-1½ pounds (450-675 g) fish scraps: head, back bone, tail, etc.
2 quarts (2 l) salted water (for fish broth)
½ small head garlic
4 tomatoes
1 onion
1-2 *jalapeños*
1-1½ pounds (450-675 g) white fish fillets

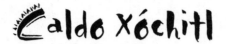aldo Xóchitl

Chicken Soup

4 chicken breasts, cut in
   halves
1 quart (1 l) chicken stock
1 onion, finely chopped
1 tablespoon (3 g) finely
   chopped cilantro leaves
2 avocados, chopped
Salt

Boil chicken breasts in a little salted water until tender. Cook down until there is just a little water. Add this water and the chicken to the quart of chicken stock.

Add the onion and cilantro, and bring to a boil.

Add the avocado, and serve with a piece of chicken breast.

Pozole Estilo Jalisco

Jalisco-Style Pozole

Boil hominy with 5 cloves garlic for 1 hour. The garlic is important in the hominy, because it makes it burst open, or flower.

Put chiles in water to cover and bring to a boil. Turn off heat.

Boil pork in enough water to cover for 1 hour with onion, garlic, salt, pepper, and oregano.

Remove the pork from water. Strain the water and mix with the hominy water. Cut meat into bite-size pieces and return to the water.

Blend chiles with a little water, and strain into the water with the meat and hominy.

Cover and simmer 1½ hours.

For the condiments, use any of the following:

> chopped radishes
> chopped onion
> lime wedges
> toasted oregano
> shredded lettuce
> crumbled tostaditas

8 pounds (3¾ kg) **hominy**
10 cloves garlic, peeled
10 *ancho* chiles, seeded
2 *guajillo* chiles, seeded
6 pounds (2¾ kg) pork head
4 pounds (2 kg) boneless pork
2 pounds (1 kg) pork back or shoulder joint
1 onion, sliced
Salt and pepper
Mucho orégano, 200 leaves

Codillo en Chilmole

Pigs Knuckle in Blackened Chile Sauce

1 pound (450 g) dry pink
  beans
2 tomatoes, chopped
1 onion, chopped
Salt
3 to 4 ounces (85-115 g)
  chilmole paste, dissolved
  in a little water or
  vinegar
¾ pound (210 g) pigs
  knuckle

Boil beans. About 1 hour before they are done, add tomatoes, onion, salt, *chilmole*, and pigs knuckle. Cook until everything is done.

It should be soupy.

Caldo de Res con Col y Garbanzos

Beef Soup with Cabbage and Garbanzos

Salt
2 teaspoons (12.4 g)
  annatto seeds
2 pounds (1 kg) beef, cut
  into ¾-inch pieces
2 tomatoes, chopped
1 onion, chopped
½ small cabbage
1 cup (250 g) cooked
  garbanzos

Add salt and annatto seeds to 3 liters boiling water. Add meat, cover, and cook until nearly done. Add pepper.

Blend the tomatoes and onion. Chop the cabbage. Add these and the garbanzos and cook until everything is done.

Mondongo

Tripe Soup

Roast the garlic, tomatoes, and onions as in recipe for iguana. Grind with cloves, cinnamon, and chiles. Fry in the oil 5 minutes.

Cut the tripe into pieces about 1-inch square and put into 2 quarts (2 l) boiling, salted water, along with the tomato mixture and bay leaves. Boil gently, covered, about 1½ hours, or until tripe is nearly done. Add the rest of the ingredients and continue cooking for ½ hour. It should be a little thicker than soup. Serve garnished with chopped parsley.

6 cloves garlic
1 pound (450 g) tomatoes
2 onions
2 cloves
⅛ teaspoon (.25 g) cinnamon
4 *jalapeño* chiles, roasted, peeled, and seeded
2 tablespoons (28 ml) oil
2 pounds (1 kg) tripe
3 bay leaves
1 15-ounce (425 g) can garbanzos, drained
12 olives
2 teaspoons (3 g) capers
Several sprigs of chopped parsley
Salt

Mondongo Andaluza

Tripe Soup with Garbanzos

2 pounds (1 k) tripe, cut
   into bite-size pieces
5 leaves oregano
1 teaspoon (4 g) black
   pepper
Salt to taste
2 chiles *xcatic*, roasted
   until blackened
3 tablespoons (45 ml)
   olive oil
½ pound (¼ kg) bacon,
   coarsely chopped
½ pound (¼ kg) raw ham,
   coarsely chopped
   (optional)
½ pound (¼ kg) chorizo,
   cut into pieces
   (optional)
6 cloves garlic, sliced
1 pound (½ kg) or more
   tomatoes, chopped
1 red bell pepper, chopped
2 pounds (1 kg) potatoes,
   cut into pieces
15-ounce (425 g) can
   garbanzos
Several sprigs parsley,
   chopped

Bring the tripe to boil, along with the spices and chiles *xcatic*, in 4 to 5 quarts (4 to 5 liters) water. Fry remaining ingredients except potatoes and garbanzos in olive oil about 15 mintues, and add to boiling tripe. Continue cooking until the tripe is done, about 2 hours.

Add the potatoes and garbanzos the last few mintues and continue cooking until the potatoes are done. Garnish with chopped parsley.

Mondongo Kabic

A Simple Tripe Soup

This is the most common recipe for Mondongo in the Yucatán, often served in *cocinas economicas*. It is also the simplest.

Put all but the last three ingredients in a pot with about 3 quarts (2¾ l) water. Bring to a boil. Cover and simmer until tripe is done, approximately 2 hours.

The tripe and calves foot are removed from the liquid and served on a plate. A bowl of the broth, the condiments, and French bread are served separately.

2 pounds (1 kg) tripe, cut into bite-sized pieces

½ pound (225 g) calves foot (can be chopped into pieces as with ham hocks)

½ sprig epazote

1 head garlic, roasted whole until blackened

1 ball allspice

1¾ ounces (50 g) *recado colorado* paste, dissolved in a little vinegar (or its equilavent if you make your own)

1 pound (½ k) tomatoes, sliced

1 onion, chopped

Salt to taste

Chopped chives

Chile *habanero*, sliced thinly

Lime wedges

Chocolomo

Fresh Beef and Organ Soup

Chocolomo is a soup that has stewing beef, kidney, liver, and heart, all cut into pieces. It is boiled in enough salted water to cover until done, about ½ to 1 hour. It is complimented with *salpicón*, a mixture of chopped radish, onion, and cilantro, sour orange, and salt.

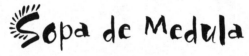

Sopa de Medula

Bone Marrow Soup

1 onion
6 Italian plum tomatoes
3 *guajillo* chiles (soaked in boiling water 15 minutes)
1 tablespoon (14 ml) oil
1 pound (450 g) marrow
1 clove garlic, chopped
1 15-ounce (425 g) can garbanzos, drained
2 teaspoons (1.2 g) powdered chicken bouillon

Blend ½ onion, tomatoes, and chile, and fry in oil for 3 minutes. Put marrow in pot with ½ onion (sliced), garlic, garbanzos, and chicken bouillon with enough water to cover, and boil for 5 minutes.

If there is tough skin on marrow, peel and return to pot.

This same soup can be made with 3 peeled and coarsely chopped potatoes in place of the marrow. It can also be made with chopped spinach.

Caldo de Res Isla Mujeres

Beef Soup from Isla Mujeres

Roast tomatoes, garlic, and onion as in recipe for iguana. Peel and smash tomatoes.

Add everything but vegetables to 4 quarts (3¾ l) boiling water.

Boil until meat is approaching done and add vegetables. Continue cooking until everything is done.

3 tomatoes
4 cloves garlic
1 medium onion
3 cloves, ground
8-10 peppercorns, ground
4 balls allspice, ground
½ teaspoon (25 g) oregano
1-inch (2½ cm) piece cinnamon, ground
3 tablespoons (45 g) powdered chicken bouillon
2 pounds (1 kg) chunks of beef with bones (or soup bones and chunks of meat)
1 or 2 *calabazas* or zucchini, coarsely chopped
3 carrots, peeled and sliced into 2 inch (5 cm) strips
3 *camotes* (if not available, 1 or 2 sweet potatoes may be substituted), coarsely chopped

Caldo de Cazón

Shark Soup

The *sopa de medula* recipe can also be made using slices of shark instead of bone marrow, 2 peeled and coarsely chopped potatoes, and *hierbas de olor*. *Hierbas de olor* include bay leaves, fresh oregano, fresh thyme, fresh parsley, fresh marjoram, and pepper. Also, fry ¼ onion before adding the tomato and chile mixture.

Ensalda de Uvas

Grape Salad

½ pound (225 g) chopped
  ham, shrimp, or a
  combination
1 large onion, chopped
1 pound (450 g) seedless
  grapes
3 strips celery, chopped
1 cup (226 g) mayonnaise
1 tablespoon (3 g)
  prepared mustard
Juice of 1 lime
1 tablespoon (12.5 g)
  sugar
3 tablespoons (42 ml)
  olive oil
Dill weed
Pepper

Mix everything together, and put in refrigerator to chill.

Huevos Revueltos con Chaya

Scrambled Eggs with Chaya

Boil the chaya for about 30 minutes. Chop and add to beaten eggs. Scramble.

Petra told me how to make *brazo de mestiza*. I had heard it called *brazo de reina*. Both this and *chaya* with scrambled eggs are often served as afternoon botanas in Yucatán restaurants and bars.

Boil the chaya, chop, and mix with *masa* flour, water, and butter or lard. Although it's not usually done, she mixes a little finely chopped ham with the *masa*. Roll the masa around a hard boiled egg near each end, and one in the middle. Petra held her hands about 8 inches (20 cm) apart to show me how long the "bar" as she called it, should be. It is then rolled in a banana leaf, like a large tamale, and steamed for about 1½ hours. A cloth can be used instead of a banana leaf.

Make a sauce of roasted tomatoes. Toast and grind squash seeds. Chop some hard-boiled eggs. Put tomato sauce over the *brazo de mestizo*, then the squash seeds, and the chopped eggs. It is then cut in slices and served.

About ¼ pound (115 g) chaya leaves, or when wadded up, about the size of a small head of cabbage (spinach can be substituted)

6 eggs

Butter or oil

Salt and pepper as you please

Huevos con Nopales

Eggs With Nopals

1 onion
1 tablespoon (14 ml) oil
6 Italian plum tomatoes
   (that is mainly what is
   sold in Yucatán markets)
2 cups (280 g) nopals (if
   preparing fresh, prepare
   as for "Fish Baked with
   Nopals". If using
   nopals in a jar, rinse.)
6 eggs, beaten
Salt

Slice onion thin. Sauté in the oil for about 2 minutes.

Chop the tomatoes and add, along with the nopals. Simmer uncovered about 10 minutes. Add eggs, stirring until done. Season to taste with salt.

Tomates de Cascara Fritos

Fried Green Tomatillos

Remove husks from tomatillos, wash, dry, and slice into ¼ inch (1 cm) thick slices. Salt and dip in the flour, egg, and breadcrumbs.

Fry in hot oil, about ⅛ inch (½ cm) deep, about 1 minute on each side, or until a light brown.

12 large tomatillos
Salt
A little flour
2 eggs, beaten
A little bit of breadcrumbs
A little oil

Tortas de Papas

Potato Patties

Boil potatoes in salted water. Mash.

Mix everything together except oil. Make into patties, and fry in oil until golden

3 large potatoes
1 egg, beaten
2 tablespoons (18 g) flour
**½ cup (55 g) grated cheese
  that melts**
Salt
Oil

Cebollas en Escabeche

Pickled Red Onions

2 red onions, thinly sliced
1 raw beet
1½ cups (337 ml) white
   vinegar
10 peppercorns
1½ teaspoon (.75 g)
   oregano
Salt
1 *jalapeño* or *habanero*
   chile, chopped

Put onions in a colander and pour boiling water over them. Peel the beet, slice it thinly, and boil in 1 cup (140 ml) water for 5 minutes. Strain.

Combine the beet water with vinegar and bring to a boil. Put onions in a container, such as a quart jar. Add peppercorns, oregano, salt, and chile.

Pour the vinegar mixture with the onions. Let sit for about 6 hours before using. It will keep a long time.

Cebollas en Escabeche 2

Red Onion with Vinegar

1 large red onion
2 tablespoons (28 ml)
   white vinegar
1 clove garlic
Couple pinches cumin
Couple pinches oregano
5 or so peppercorns
Salt

Chop onions coarsely, or slice thinly and cut through center. Put in a small pan and pour over boiling water. Drain immediately. Add vinegar, crushed garlic, cumin, oregano, peppercorns, and salt. Bring to a boil and remove from heat. This is a very common Yucatán garnish served with meat and poultry and will keep for days.

Ensalada de Calabazas

Summer Squash Salad

Cook the squash in water with salt and baking soda. When cooked and cooled, slice and arrange on a platter. Mash the egg yolks with vinegar. Add oil, salt, pepper, parsley, mustard, and mix well. Pour over the squash. Sprinkle with finely chopped egg whites and cheese. This is best served chilled the following day.

1 pound (680 g) small summer squash (yellow squash are good)
1 teaspoon (3.3 g) baking soda
3 hard boiled eggs
1 cup (225 ml) white vinegar
6 tablespoons (84 ml) olive oil
Salt and pepper to taste
A few sprigs parsley, finely chopped
1 teaspoon (5 g) French mustard
2 ounces (60 g) shredded or crumbled mozzarella or other white cheese

Vegetarian Indian Stuffed Peppers

1 small onion, finely
  chopped
Oil
2 cloves garlic, minced
1 teaspoon (2 g) cumin
2 teaspoons (10 g) grated
  ginger
½ teaspoon (2 g) cayenne
  pepper
¼ teaspoon (.5 g) turmeric
3 potatoes, boiled and
  mashed
4 ounces (80 g) sesame
  seeds, toasted and
  crushed
1½ teaspoons (.75 g) salt
6 bell peppers
1 lime or lemon
Yogurt

Fry the onion in oil until lightly browned. Add the garlic and spices, and fry for 3 minutes. Mix with the mashed potatoes, sesame seeds, and salt.

Cut down the side of the peppers, and remove seeds. Stuff with mashed potato mixture, and fry in oil for about 5 minutes.

Put lime or lemon juice over the peppers, cover, and simmer until tender. It may be necessary to add a little water.

Serve with yogurt.

Coliflor con Queso

Cauliflower With Cheese Sauce

Quarter the cauliflower and cook in salted water.

Put 3½ ounces (100 g) butter and flour in a pan and heat over a low flame. Blend. Add milk, salt, onion, carrots, and crushed cloves. Cook, stirring often, until it begins to thicken. Add the beaten egg yolks and pepper, and blend thoroughly. Stir in 3½ ounces (100 g) grated cheese. When the mixture begins to boil, turn the heat off. Remove the onion and carrot pieces from the sauce and pour the sauce over the cauliflower in a buttered baking dish. Sprinkle the rest of the cheese and breadcrumbs on top and bake at about 300° until golden brown, about 20-30 minutes.

1 large cauliflower
5 ounces (140 g) butter
3½ tablespoons (30 g) flour
1 quart (1 l) milk
Salt
1 large onion, cut in half
2 carrots, sliced length wise
2 cloves, crushed
3 egg yolks, beaten
½ tablespoon (1.65 g) ground pepper
5 ounces (140 g) grated cheese
2 tablespoons (15 g) breadcrumbs

Bróculi capeado

Breaded, Fried Broccoli

2 pounds (1 kg) broccoli
½ pound (225 g) cheese
   that melts
2 eggs
Flour
Breadcrumbs
Oil
Salt

Cut broccoli into pieces that have fairly thick stems so you can wedge slices of cheese into them. Boil 5 minutes. Separate eggs, and beat whites until fluffy. Beat yolks and stir in. Slice cheese and put it where the broccoli has been cut open.

Dip in flour, egg, and breadcrumbs. Fry in hot oil about 1inch (2 cm) deep, turning until brown.

Broccoli *capeado* is served like this or with chile pasilla sauce.

hile Pasilla

Chile Pasilla Paste

5 pasilla chiles
2 Italian plum tomatoes
1 small onion
Salt

Prepare the chiles as in *a la diabla* sauce. Blend the tomatoes and onion. Heat and mix. Pour over the broccoli, or serve on the side.

Ensalada de Nopalitos

Nopal Salad

Cook the nopals with avocado leaves in salted water 30 to 40 minutes, until they don't squeak.

Roast chiles in a dry pan about 10 minutes. Devein, seed, and slice into thin strips.

Salt and mix everything together. Good served cold with a little olive oil mixed in.

1 pound (450 g) nopals
avocado leaves (optional)
¼ pound (115 g) tomatoes, chopped
Sal, al gusto
Serrano **chiles,** *al gusto*
1 small onion, cut in half and thinly sliced
Cilantro *al gusto*

Nopales en Escabeche

Marinated Nopal

5 nopal leaves, spines
    removed, and cut in
    strips about ¼ inch (1
    cm) x ¾ inch (1½ cm)
4 or 5 *jalapeño* chiles
5 peppercorns, or ¼ tea
    spoon (1 g) black
    pepper
2 cloves
2 onions, sliced and cut in
    half
4 cloves garlic, minced
¼ teaspoon (.5 g) basil
⅛ teaspoon (.25 g) thyme
1 cup (225 ml) vinegar
⅓ cup (83 ml) oil
Salt

Boil nopal strips in salted water for 20 minutes. Cut the chiles in strips, removing veins and seeds. Grind peppers and cloves.

Put everything in a pot and simmer for about 15 minutes, until chiles and nopals are tender and *don't* squeak.

Nopales Rellenos

Stuffed Nopals

Boil nopals in salted water until done. Leave whole. Spread cheese, onion, chile, and tomato over a nopal leaf, and put another leaf over it.

Fry each side in very hot oil until cheese melts.

2 nopals, spines removed, for each "sandwich"

4-5 tablespoons (30-40 g) grated Oaxacan cheese (or any substitute you wish)

2 or 3 thin slices onion for each "sandwich"

½ *jalapeño* for every "sand-wich"

2 thin slices tomato for each "sandwich"

⅛ inch (1 cm) oil in bottom of pan

Budín de Nopales

Nopal Casserole

1 onion, chopped
Oil
8 nopals, prepared as
above and chopped
1 pound (450 g) Oaxaca
cheese, shredded
2 tomatoes, chopped
3 sprigs epazote

Sauté onion in oil until just soft. Grease a casserole dish. Put in a layer of chopped nopals, followed by shredded cheese, onion, tomato, and epazote leaves. Repeat.

Put in 350° (180°C) oven for 20 minutes.

Frijoles Negros

Village Style Black Beans

1 pound (450 g) black
beans
1 onion, chopped
1 or 2 garlic cloves,
minced
1 tablespoon (5 g) epazote
(stems can be used)

Cook the beans with the other ingredients. Let them cook down and mash with a spoon so there will be a sort of bean sauce mixed with whole beans.

Frijoles Charros

Ranch Style Beans

Boil beans in water. When they are almost done, add the bacon and chorizo, and simmer 25 minutes.

Add the onion, tomato, and cilantro, and simmer 5 minutes. Add salt to taste.

½ pound (225 g) dried kidney beans
2 strips bacon, chopped
8 inches (20 cm) chorizo, chopped
1 onion, chopped
3 tomatoes, chopped
2 tablespoons (6.2 g) chopped cilantro
Salt

Calabazas Rellenas

Squash Stuffed with Pork

½ **pound (225 g) lean
   ground pork**
Oil
½ **onion, chopped**
2 cloves garlic, minced
2 *jalapeño* chiles, chopped
**1 teaspoon (1 g) dried
   basil**
1 teaspoon (.5 g) salt
**1 teaspoon (3.3 g) coarsely
   ground black pepper**
**2 tablespoons (28 ml)
   wine vinegar**
3 tomatoes, chopped
**6 squash, about 3 inches
   (8 cm) across**
Shredded cheese

Sauté pork with onion, garlic, and spices until done. Stir in the wine vinegar. Roast tomatoes 15 minutes in a frying pan or *comal*. Peel and smash in a *molcajete*. Remove tops of squash and scoop out pulp. Chop the pulp and combine with meat mixture.

Fill the squash. Put the tomatoes on top, then the shredded cheese, and bake in a 350° (180°C) oven 15 to 20 minutes.

THE ESTRELLAS

It seems that things are more likely to go wrong at home when one has gone away for a couple of days: things like food spoiling faster and the likelihood of someone dying whom you will especially miss. But trouble is not confined to back home. Things like cars and teeth can develop minds of their own when they enter a foreign country. It would seem that a Fiat would have a very low IQ, but mine was as smart as a whip. One time when I drove it to southern Mexico, the engine failed within fifty miles of the border.

The last time I drove to southern Mexico, it was my teeth. They were not as vindictive as the Fiat had been; they waited until they had crossed the Tropic of Cancer before they began to release their fillings. It was not because of more than normal abuse, such as being asked to grind a hard piece of *chicharrón*. It was because they were in Mexico and knew they were going to be there for a while. But, thanks to my teeth, I had the good fortune of becoming friends with Doña María and her family.

When I arrived in Mérida, I went to a dentist who had been recommended to me. His helper, Ricardo, had recently graduated from dental school and had begun his internship in social service working on the teeth of people who could not afford a private dentist. During a visit one day in mid-September, he invited me to spend Independence Day (September 16) with him. We would go to his girlfriend Elda's house in Mérida for *pozole* in the afternoon, then to his parents' house that night. Having spent the previous Independence Day in Gringo Gulch, I was eager to see how the local people celebrated the occasion.

Independence Day in Colonía García Gínerez

By the time Ricardo and I arrived at Elda's house, a crowd had already gathered. Many people were standing because there were not enough chairs to go around. Most of them were either members of the Estrella family or in-laws.

Three generations of the family lived in two houses on the same piece of property, but they came and went as though the dwellings were one home. Officially, Doña María and her husband Don Manuel lived in the house in which the party was being held. Manuela—their oldest living daughter—

79

and her husband Enrique lived in the other house with their four daughters, Veronica, Sarah, Mary, and Elda. I lost track of people after being introduced to Socorro, Manuel, and María's youngest daughter, her husband Beto, and their two children.

Doña María, a petite woman, is about four feet, one inch tall. She has white hair, a weathered face, and a warm smile. In a *huipil,* she looks like a postcard come to life in the form of a large doll. Doña María is seventy-six years old although she looks about eighty-five. Manuel, often called Papie, has the somewhat slanted forehead characteristic of the Maya and is not much taller than his wife.

María was busy chopping condiments for the *pozole* when we arrived. Manuela and Socorro were getting it ready to serve. It had been cooked in a large pot over an open fire behind the house. People both standing and sitting were having *botanas.* Using either toothpicks or chips, in customary Yucatecan style, they were eating boiled potatoes with pig's ears, a dish known as *papas con orejas* (p. 7). The table that held the *botanas* was in the kitchen, which opened directly into the backyard. Everyone but the children was drinking beer in glasses. Doña María toasted me, as did the rest of the family. To them a toast is not simply a matter of raising glasses; the glasses must touch.

As soon as I was served my bowl of *pozole,* several family members showed me how to prepare it for eating—which ingredients to add and how much of each. Don Manuel told me to watch as he ritualistically crumbled tortilla chips in his hand and mixed them into his bowl; he then watched to make sure I was doing it correctly. All the condiments, oregano, chopped chili, lime, and tortilla chips were passed to me at least once. All the while the focus of attention was on my bowl of *pozole.* It was important that the gringo had it right.

Doña María was the last to be seated at the table. Fortunately, a seat had been left for her. When I accepted an offer of a second bowl of *pozole,* it was she who got up for it. I tried to get it myself, not wanting her to bother, but she had obviously been "bothering" for many years; it seemed to be part of her mission in life. As she reached high into the pot, the serving spoon looked like a sand shovel in the hands of a small child.

When everyone had finished eating, Manuela told me how to make the *botana* and the *pozole.* She said this *pozole* was red because it contained *ancho* and *guajillo* chiles. It's called *pozole estilo Jalisco* (p. 57). *Pozole* is a popular dish in Yucatán.

Doña María began to reminisce about the cooking in her hometown of Tamek, about twenty-five miles east of Mérida. She said the people there used to eat *tuzas* and *topos* which, by her description, I would guess to be gophers and moles. The villagers would either boil them or baste them with *recado colorado* and grill them over charcoal. They cooked armadillo the same way, though sometimes they would cut the meat off the bones, cover it with *recado colorado,* and bake it in the shell for about an hour and a half. It is not uncommon to see Maya women sitting on roadside rocks with a couple of live armadillos for sale.

María went on to tell me some of her kitchen magic. Whenever food begins sticking to the pot, she said, put orange peel under the cooking vessel. If the food is too salty, pour salt on top of the lid, and continue boiling. To tenderize boiling meat, add to the pot a chip of ice, a piece of broken plate, or a nail; when using a nail, it is wise to put it into a cork so it will not get lost or forgotten. When adding salt or bones to a pot of broth, placing them in the shape of a cross on the surface of the liquid will stave off bad luck. I mentioned that Alberto kept scissors opened in the shape of a cross when he was not using them.

"That is to keep the *aluxes* away," María explained.

Aluxes, I knew, were mean little troll-like creatures that hide people's belongings or move them from one room to another. Out in the country they are even worse—they steal corn. The crossed scisssors is good to know; *Aluxes* are a plague everywhere I have ever been.

Later, I tried one of María's tips by purposely oversalting a pot of *frijoles* and pouring salt on the lid. When they were done, they were so salty I had to cook a pot of unsalted beans and mix them together. This worked. Perhaps the problem was that I did not believe. I could visualize myself riding in and out of Lourdes in a wheelchair, my disbelief standing in the way of a cure.

I asked María if she used to make *chocolomo* (fresh beef and organ soup) (p. **00**) in Tamek. She said she did. The soup should be made with fresh meat, she told me, on the day the cow is butchered. The stewing beef, kidney, liver, and heart are all cut into bite-size pieces, then boiled in salted water to cover until done.

"About how long?" I asked.

"I don't know . . . until it's done. It depends on the fire and the pot," she replied.

"About one and a half hours," Manuela interjected. Manuela, in her forties, was the first of María's children to be born in Mérida.

While the women cleaned up, the men sat and talked. Beto worked for Pemex, Mexico's government-owned oil company. On business trips he had learned about the cooking styles of Guerrero and Michoacán, coastal states in southern Mexico. While some of the other men tried to teach me nasty words in Maya, Beto recited wonderful recipes. I have forgotten the nasty words, but the recipes I remember well. They were for *puerco frito estilo Guerrero* (fried pork ribs) (p. 115), *costillas de res estilo Guerrero* (boiled beef ribs) (p. 100), and *pescado a la talla* (fish grilled with achiote) (p. 176).

Soon it came time for Ricardo and me to leave and go visit his parents. That night *carne asada* was served. They grilled thin slices of pork and beef that had been marinated in lime. I had never before heard pork referred to as *carne asada*. After the meat was cooked, it was cut into thin strips and served with tortillas. A red chile sauce, a guacamole sauce, and coarsely chopped onion were passed around to put on top of the tacos.

Ricardo's mother was from Veracruz. When I told her how much I enjoyed *pescado a la Veracruzana,* she explained that it was served throughout Mexico, but in Veracruz the same method is used to cook other seafood, such as octopus, shrimp, and crab. *Ancho* chiles are used abundantly in Veracruz, she added, and the cooking is hot. She then gave me recipes for *sopa de ostión con chile ancho* (oyster soup with chile *ancho* (p. 51), *pulpo con tomate* (octopus with tomatoes) (p. 201), *pescado en adobo* (fish sautéed in chile sauce) (p. 177) *sopa de jaiba con chilpachole* (crab with sauce) (p. 199), *chilpachole de jaiba* (crab soup with chile ancho) (p. 53), and *quesadillas de pescado veracruzana* (fish quesadillas) (p. 186).

Gallipava

On my next visit to the dentist, I asked Ricardo if he thought Doña María would cook a turkey with *recado colorado,* provided that I brought the bird. He said he would find out and let me know.

The Estrellas, it turned out, would be glad to prepare this dish the following Sunday. So I went in search of a bird. Instead of a turkey, I bought a *gallipava. Gallipava* is a Yucatán term for a type of chicken that is as large as a small turkey.

Doña María greeted me at the door. In addition to the *gallipava,* I had brought a bag containing achiote paste for the *recado colorado,* as well as two six-packs of Tecate. I told her I had *chivos* in the bag—unintentionally mispronouncing the plural of *cheva,* a slang term for *cerveza* that they had taught me. Doña María let out a hearty cackle, then hurried to tell the other family members what I had said. In my confusion, I had told her I had goats in the bag.

She unwrapped the bird, smelled it, and wrinkled her nose. Manuela smelled it and asked where I got it. When I told her, she said, "Never buy meat from there. That's the worst market in Mérida."

The two women took the *gallipava* to a sink in the backyard. They washed it thoroughly with water, then gave it two good scrubbings with lime juice. The *gallipava* was rejuvenated.

Manuela put the bird in a large pot with water to cover and brought it to a boil. Doña María added 5 cloves of roasted garlic, about 1 teaspoon of pepper, 1 teaspoon of dried oregano leaves, and 3 teaspoons of salt. In two and a half hours, we would be sitting down to *gallipava asado.*

While the *gallipava* was boiling, we took a break for *botanas* and beer. Manuela set a bowl of tortilla chips on the table, and María made *hasikilpac* (p. 23), a squash seed dip for the chips. I watched her each step of the way and enjoyed the dip so much that she said I would be the one to make it next time.

When the *gallipava* had boiled 1¼ hours, it was set on a platter, ready for basting. The *recado colorado* was simple to prepare. Doña María began by spooning ¼ pound of the achiote paste into a *molcajete* I had brought. I had purchased it at the market where *recado* mongers sell homemade red, black, and greenish pastes for *recado colorado, chilmole,* and *pipián* dishes, respectively. I asked María if the red paste I had selected was better than the store-bought brands.

"*Si,*" she said. "*Es mas alegre, viva mas*" ("It is more cheerful, more alive").

She proceeded to mix the achiote paste with vinegar—just enough to form the consistency of a thick gravy. The mixture was then used for basting the bird, both inside and out. The basted *gallipava* was set on a grill over hot charcoal and turned about every 15 minutes. After 1¼ hours, it was pronounced done. The bird was a pretty red-brown color all over.

Accompanying the *gallipava* were tortillas, black beans that had been mashed to a paste with a large spoon, lettuce, a bowl of sliced onions and tomatoes, and a bowl of sliced white onion in vinegar. Also served were *longaniza de Valladolid* (a Yucatecan chorizo-like sausage) that had been heated over the coals and a soup that had been made by boiling macaroni in the *gallipava* broth. The table was so crowded with food that plates were overlapping. The fact that the bottom of one was sticking to the black beans caused no consternation. Although forks lay here and there, they were not used much. Spoons, however, were passed around for the soup. The plate of *longaniza* was set in front of Doña María, seemingly because that was the only available space. Hence, that is mainly what she ate. It is not in vogue to worry about cholesterol in the Yucatán.

Nor is it customary to worry about the transfer of germs from hands to food. Doña María had used her hands to peel and smash the boiled tomatoes for the *hasikilpac* and to mix them with the other ingredients. She had used the same method to prepare the *recado*. But because she and her family were so likable, this hands-on method made no difference to me. Germ theory, I concluded, must hinge somewhat on psychological realities.

Partway through dinner, Beto announced that he had acquired a large piece of venison from a pueblo in Quintana Roo.

"Isn't there a large fine for killing a deer?" I asked.

"Not only that," he replied, "but you go to jail."

Deer hunting had not always been considered a crime in the Yucatán. The first time I was in Mérida in 1972, venison appeared regularly on restaurant menus. But as years passed, the deer were overkilled, and penalties against killing them were instated. Now, although venison is no longer served in restaurants in Mérida, it is sometimes sold "under the table" in the market. And it is still available in pueblos and sometimes in out-of-the-way restaurants and cantinas.

I was invited to return the following Sunday for *pipián de venado* (Venison stew with squash seeds), a formerly legal Yucatecan specialty. This time I was asked to bring *cebollinas* (chives) and cilantro and to make *hasikilpac*, now that I knew how. Doña María and Don Manuel would supply the rest of the ingredients.

Onsiquil, A Venison Dinner

When I arrived at 9:30 in the morning, Doña María and Socorro were in the backyard. María was cleaning the hindquarter of a deer. Socorro was in her church clothes and about to leave, which meant that her mother would have to finish the cleaning without her. Even so, as was María's custom, she would not let me help.

To make matters worse, I had come empty-handed. While gathering my ingredients for the *hasikilpac* earlier that morning, I noticed that the *cebollinas* had not made it home from the supermarket, and the cilantro had turned to mush. Foods spoil fast in the tropics, even when their owners are watching them. Papie came to the rescue. He said he would try to find the herbs, since he was going for tomatoes anyway. He often rides his bicycle to stores and houses around the neighborhood to get ingredients needed in the kitchen.

María, meanwhile, finished cleaning the deer, put the bones and less tender cuts of meat into a large pot, and carried it to the stove. Again she would not let me help; she is a strong little woman, I reminded myself, and has no apparent back problems after all these years of arduous labor. Next, María added water to the pot by reaching up and pouring in several smaller potfuls, one after another. She sprinkled about 1 tablespoon of salt into the palm of her hand, tossed it into the pot, then added about 1 teaspoon of pepper and 5 leaves of oregano. She reached up and began feeling around on the shelf near the stove. I asked what she was looking for. It was only after I asked that she said she needed help to reach the garlic. She thanked me, peeled 4 cloves of the garlic, and smashed them with a stone on a *metate* before adding them to the pot. Then she brought everything to a vigorous boil.

Papie returned with only tomatoes. After delivering them, he prepared to set off again for the *cebollinas* and cilantro, which I knew would be at least a mile-long excursion. He accepted a ride in my truck. Having me drive Papie to the market was okay with Doña María, who allowed me three forms of work: reaching for ingredients on the high shelf, going to the market, and fetching her a beer from time to time. As for Papie, although he spends much of his time at home in a rocking chair, he is far from confined to it. He, like Alberto, makes getting old seem bright.

During our ride, Papie broke down the Maya word *hasikilpac* into Spanish for me. "ha," he said, means water; "sikil" means squash seeds; and "pac" means tomato. He told me that in the pueblos, *hasikilpac* is sometimes rolled in tortillas for a main course. Other times, tortillas are spread with only the crushed, toasted *pepita*.

Lessons in Maya linguistics are easy to come by in certain circles of the Yucatán. Never having stayed more than a few weeks on previous visits, I had not realized the extent of Maya influence on the larger culture, and I had considered the language nearly as dead as Latin. But I was to learn that in the pueblos, Maya continues to coexist with Spanish and that even young people speak both languages. Elsewhere, they coexist because of tourism, other businesses, the *cinema,* and the *parabólica* (satellite dish). English has replaced Maya as the second most important language. Still, the Maya people are proud of their heritage, and people in the cities like to flaunt whatever native Maya phrases they may know.

Papie and I stocked up on the missing ingredients. When we got back, María gave me a knife and a cutting board so I could begin chopping the *cebollinas.* Her husband sharpened another knife and handed it to me with a smile, explaining that if I cut myself with this one, it would not hurt. I thanked him and began chopping.

María set to work on the *pipián* (squash seed sauce). First she placed on the table two large pots, a colander, and a *jícara;* this dried gourd, cut in half to make a round-bottomed bowl, was filled with water. In one of the pots she mixed about ½ pound of toasted and ground *pepita* with enough water to form a thick liquid. To this she added about 12 ounces of achiote paste. She was meticulous, smashing between her thumb and fingers every lump she found. She then poured the entire mixture into the colander, pressing it through the perforations and into the second pot. To the reddish earthen-colored substance that remained, she added small amounts of water until the colander contained only squash seed husks. She repeated this step one more time, using a finer strainer. (The ground *pepita* I used in the *hasikilpac* remained unstrained, so all *those* husks are eaten rather than thrown away.)

After boiling for ½ hour, the venison was removed from the stock, which was then poured into a large clay pot. The *pipián* was stirred in and the boiled meat added. The stew was left to simmer another 45 minutes.

All attention was then turned to the choice meat, which was to be served separately. It was sliced into thin steaks, covered with lime juice, and simmered with the lid on in a little oil for ½ hour.

Doña María, having a little time to relax, put on her glasses. It was the first time I had seen her wear them. She said that sometimes her eyes get tired and tears come out. Although she was full of energy, I could tell that her age occasionally caught up with her. Very quietly she asked if I wanted a *lata*—a word that means "can" and, in this case, "can of beer." I got one for each of us. Returning, I noticed a napkin wrapped around one of María's fingers, which she had apparently cut. She unwrapped it to show me her wound. I marveled at how alike people are, regardless of their age or the part of the world they live. She toasted me with her can of beer and gave me a broad and radiant smile.

Little by little, more people trickled in: Socorro and her family, the party responsible for the venison, Manuela and her family, who were always there, and a few parents and siblings of in-laws. Although this Sunday was not a holiday, the venison dinner had made it a special occasion.

I was the first to be given a bowl of the *pipián de venado*. A fork, knife, and spoon had been set at my place; however, I was told to use my fingers for the bones. The spoon was for the liquid and the fork and knife for the steaks. Everything was extraordinarily good, including the *hasikilpac*.

After dinner, I looked in the refrigerator for the beer but could not find any. Manuela showed me that she had hidden them in the vegetable compartment. Nodding toward the next room, she indicated that she was keeping them away from her mother, or perhaps her father, or perhaps Socorro's father-in-law, or maybe all of them.

As family members began leaving for home, María became sleepy. Manuela came to sit beside her. At such times, Manuela nestles close to her mother so she can catch her if she happens to fall asleep. María sits with her elbows propped on the table and her head in her hands, trying to stay alert. When she dozes off, she wakes with a start and laughs at herself. A more pleasant Maya grandmother would be hard to find.

Hana Pixan—*Día de los Muertos*—Day of the Dead

The Day of the Dead is an ancient Maya festival that begins at midnight on the 31st of October, a day celebrated elsewhere as Halloween. In honor of the occasion, people throughout Mexico make altars in their homes and place on them pictures of deceased loved ones, along with some of their favorite foods and beverages. The 1st of November through the 8th—a week known in Maya as *Hana Pixan* and in Spanish as *Comer Ánimas*—commemorates an interlude in which souls of the dead return to eat and drink. Pueblo dwellers believe that the visiting souls stay for the entire month of November. The 1st of November is traditionally a children's celebration; the 2nd is for adults, although in practice this does not seem to be the case. I was told that fruit and candies that children like are consumed on the first and adult items such as liquor on the second.

The food prepared for this occasion varies from place to place. In

Mérida, *mucbil pollo* (buried-rock chicken) is served on the 1st of November. In the pueblos, *pavo en relleno negro* (turkey stuffed with ground pork in blackened chile sauce) is served on the 1st, followed by *mucbil pollo* and *pib de espelón* on the 8th.

The Estrellas invited me to spend the 1st of November with them to watch as they prepared *mucbil pollo.* By 7:00 AM when I arrived bearing Tecate, much of the meal preparation had already been completed. In addition, an altar had been made, displaying a crucifix, burning candles, and a picture of the Virgin. A photograph of María and Manuel's oldest daughter, who had died five months earlier, was fastened by a clothespin to a little stand on the altar. *Pan de los muertos* (bread of the dead) had also been placed on the altar, along with cookies, crackers, candy, a pitcher of hot chocolate, and another of *atole nuevo,* a thick, sweet white drink made with young corn.

Soon after I arrived, I was served hot chocolate and *pan de los muertos.* The *pan* varies from region to region throughout Mexico. In Mexico City, it is flavored with cinnamon and sugar; in the state of Yucatán, it is only slightly sweet. Papie opened a can of Tecate and put it on the altar. He explained that the *pan, atole,* and chocolate were traditional Day of the Dead foods, whereas the others on the altar were favorites of the deceased. Papie went on to say that a dead cousin who had liked beer was being honored by the Tecate. His oldest daughter had liked *aguardiente* (rum-like cane liquor), so there was a bottle of that next to her picture.

The kitchen was bustling with activity. A large pot of water was simmering on the stove. The liquid was a reddish color because *recado colorado* had been boiling in it, along with 6½ pounds of pork backbone added for flavor. The meat was then cut into small pieces. In other pots fourteen quartered chickens were boiled in shifts. Everything could not be cooked at once, even though all family members over the age of seventeen were helping.

The table was covered with 55 pounds of *masa* (tortilla dough). Three pounds of melted pork lard were then slowly kneaded into the *masa,* together with a rather large amount of salt. After more kneading, Doña María broke off a little ball of dough, pulled it in half, and handed me a piece to get my opinion on whether or not it needed more salt. To my taste, it did not.

This *mucbil pollo* was serious business, undoubtedly the most arduous cooking of the year. It took two people about half an hour to knead the flour before it was pronounced mixed. Then it was formed into balls, each about 6 inches in diameter. A hole was poked by finger into each ball. Reddish lard that had been sautéed with toasted achiote seeds and strained was poured into each hole and kneaded into the ball.

The chicken, meanwhile, was picked, and the meat and bones mixed together. The necks and feet were kept separate.

Elda brought out a bowl of *xec* she had prepared. *Xec,* which is Maya for "mixed," is also traditional on the Day of the Dead. It is usually made with *jícama,* orange and grapefruit slices, chile, chopped cilantro, and salt. Elda's, however, included mandarin orange slices and had chile powder in lieu of the fresh chile.

Alberto makes a more elaborate *xec.* He uses *jícama* and the same fruits, but adds onions. These he slices thinly, cuts diagonally, and marinates, along with chopped *jalapeño* or *serrano* chiles, in sour orange or lime juice for 3 hours. He then mixes everything together.

Many Mexicans like to personalize their side dishes. *Pico de gallo,* a relish known throughout Mexico, usually consists simply of chopped *serrano* chiles, onion, and salt. A friend of Alberto's in Acapulco, however, makes a *pico de gallo* using papaya just before it ripens. Like *xec,* this dish is eaten as a *botana.* She chops and marinates the papaya in lime juice a few minutes to overnight. Then she mixes it with salt and chopped *jícama,* onion, *serrano* chiles, and cilantro.

In the back yard, work continued on the main course. Banana leaves were pulled from their center vein. Each vein was then stripped apart to make strings. The pieces of banana leaves—the largest of which measured about 6 by 12 inches—were cleaned with a wet cloth before being placed crosswise, one over the other, on the table. The open areas between the overlapping leaves were filled in with smaller pieces of leaf.

In the middle of each group of banana leaves, a *masa* ball was shaped into what looked like a 9-inch pie crust with tall sides. The pork, chicken meat, and chicken bones were layered inside. Over this was spread a red *kol.* The *kol* had been prepared by mixing into the strained meat stock 20 Italian tomatoes and 10 onions, all of which had been chopped and fried. Sprinkled over the *kol,* topping some of these filled shells, was a little chopped *habanero.*

The *masa* was worked more until it was able to be closed on top, resembling a cake. The banana leaves were then folded over the top and tied perpendicularly, like a package, with string from the center rib. Portions containing the *habanero* were marked with a bottle cap slipped under the string.

Most of the *pibs* (dishes cooked underground) were filled with the pork, chicken meat, and bone mixture. Others contained only the chicken feet and necks. These parts are considered the most tasty parts and are reserved for special friends and family.

One large piece of *masa* had been reserved to make *pib de espelón.* Sold fresh in Yucatecan markets, *espelón* are small beans that vary in color from green to nearly black. For this *pib,* about ¾ pound of *espelón* had been soaked in salted water for several hours. These were now mixed into the *masa* and wrapped like the other *pibs.*

Soon afterward, Don Manuel and I drove about a mile to the *pib* (the pit in which *pibs* are cooked) to light the fire. He told me that this was the last year he would be fooling with the *pib,* that he was getting arthritis; then he laughed and explained that he says the same thing every year. I could see he had worked hard to prepare the *pib* for cooking the *mucbil pollo.* Sticks had been cut to fit across the hole in the ground and crosshatched to support a large pile of rocks. The rocks, placed neatly in the center, formed a mound measuring about 16 by 16 by 24 inches. In the hole was dry wood to help ignite the fire.

By November, the rainy season is drawing to a close in the Mexican tropics, but just as Papie's fire started burning, a hard rain came down. He looked dejected, then propped a piece of tin over the fire. The downpour did not last long, and the fire was saved. Relieved, we drove back to the house to gather the food.

Altogether, twenty-five *pibs* were waiting on boards to be transported to the open pit. We loaded the boards into my truck and Ricardo's station wagon and set off. María and Veronica accompanied me in the truck; Elda rode with Ricardo; the remaining members of the two households rode with Enrique in the family car. We were all eager to see the cooking of the *mucbil pollo.*

By the time we reached the fire, the wood had collapsed and the hot rocks had fallen into the hole. Papie scooped a few of them aside with a shovel, then he flattened the pile of rocks in the hole and covered them with tin. The *pibs* were set on the tin. Immediately afterward, the rocks

Papie had flung aside were broken with a hammer and the pieces shoveled on top of the *pibs*. Over these were placed leaves from a *roble* (oak) tree— orange or avocado leaves may also be used—creating a great deal of smoke. More tin was added, which nearly sealed the hole. The few remaining places that allowed for the escape of smoke were covered with flour sacks and shovels of dirt. For the next 1¼ hours while the *pibs* were cooking, we sat nearby on concrete blocks talking, laughing, and drinking beer.

When the *pibs* were ready, they were returned to the house the same way they had come, and the boards on which they sat were put in the backyard. The family returned as well. As soon as other family members and in-laws began arriving, some of the *pibs* were opened. Doña María cut them into pieces like cake and distributed them by hand. A tomato and onion sauce was passed around to pour over the *espelón*. The *xec* and *pibs*, especially those containing the *mucbil pollo,* were devoured with relish.

It is a privilege to have seen *mucbil pollo* cooked and eaten as it might have been a long time ago and to have felt so at home with an unusually warm family on a day that is so special to them. They are indeed *estrellas*.

CARNES

Despite being so close to the ocean, many varieties of meat are eaten in the Yucatán. The variety of ways to prepare meat that are presented in this section shows the richness of the culinary tradition.

Amarillo de Res

Beef Stew with Chile Guajillo and Masa

3 *chayotes*
Salt
6 *guajillo* chiles
8 *chiles de árbol*
3 cloves
4 cloves garlic
1 tablespoon (14 ml) oil
2 pounds (1 kg) beef
2 ounces (60 g) *masa*
1 onion, chopped
½ pound (225 g) green
　beans, snapped
4 balls black pepper,
　ground
¾ teaspoon (.35 g) oregano
½ teaspoon (1 g) cumin
⅛ teaspoon (.25 g)
　cinnamon

Peel *chayotes* and chop into about 12 pieces each. Boil in salted water 20 minutes. Prepare chiles as in recipe for iguana.

Grind cloves, garlic, chiles, and fry in oil until onion is soft.

Boil meat, covered, in 1 quart (1 l) salted water for ½ hour. Take 1 cup (225 ml) of the broth, let cool, and mix the *masa* flour into it.

Add remaining ingredients and simmer until meat is done, about ½ hour, depending on the cut of meat. In Mexico it can take hours.

Carne de Res con Tomate

Strips of Beef with Tomato Sauce

Cut the meat into strips or small, thin slices. Mash 2 or 3 cloves garlic with the pepper, oregano, cumin, and salt. Mix them with juice from the lime. Cover the meat with this mixture. This can be left to marinate up to several days, but it is not necessary.

Grind the chile, tomatoes, onion, and a clove or two of garlic together. This can be done in a blender. Pour this tomato sauce over the meat in a pan, cover and simmer until nearly done, about 45 minutes depending on cut and thickness of meat. Remove the cover and continue simmering until the meat is done and the sauce has reduced so that it is rich and thick.

This was served with rice, black beans, summer squash salad, tortillas, and French-style bread. The salsa on the Yucatán table is the hottest I have ever had.

1 pound (½ kg) boneless beef
4 or 5 cloves garlic
1 teaspoon (3.3 kg) black pepper, ground
½ teaspoon (.3 g) or 2 good pinches oregano
2 pinches cumin
Salt
1 large lime
1 fresh, mild chile
5 or 6 tomatoes
1 large onion

Carne de Res en Escabeche

Beef with Pickled Red Onion

1 pound (450 g) boneless
 beef
1 clove garlic
5 cloves, smashed or
 ground
A couple pinches cumin
A couple pinches oregano
Vinegar
1 mild chile
2 tablespoons (30 g)
 butter
Pickled red onion
½ teaspoon (1.5 g) or so
 pepper
Salt

Cut meat into thin slices or strips. Crush the garlic and mix with the cloves, cumin, oregano, and vinegar. Pour this mixture on the meat and let marinate for a few minutes or up to several days. Broil for 3 or 4 minutes or cook over a grill. Roast the chile until it blisters, about 5 minutes. This can be done in the oven, broiler, or on a grill. Let it cool in a plastic or paper bag for a few minutes so it can be peeled easily.

If the meat is already tender after broiling (depending on the cut), put it, its juice (if any), the butter, the chile, and the pickled onion in a pan and simmer for a couple minutes, making sure that it doesn't simmer too long so that the meat gets tough. If the meat is tough after broiling, put it and all the other ingredients except the onions in a covered pan to simmer until tender. Add a little water or butter, if necessary, to keep from going dry. Put the pickled onion in during the last 5 minutes.

Carne de Res con Yema

Beef with Egg Yolk

Heat the spices in a pan with a little water. Cut the meat into thin slices or strips, put in the pan with the spices, cover and let simmer. Mince the chile, onion, parsley, crush the garlic, and fry them in the butter. Add this mixture to the meat. In a little juice from the meat and a dash of vinegar, mash the egg yolks and mix until smooth. When the meat is done, add the egg yolk mixture and let simmer a few minutes.

It is ready to serve.

1 teaspoon (3.3 g) pepper
2 pinches oregano
3 cloves, ground or
   crushed
A couple of pinches cumin
A couple of good pinches
   saffron
A couple of good pinches
   coriander seeds
1 pound (450 g)
   boneless beef
1 mild chile
1 onion
2 or 3 sprigs parsley
3 cloves garlic
2 tablespoons (30 g)
   butter
Salt
Dash vinegar
3 yolks or hard-boiled
eggs

Cuete Mechado

Rolled Stuffed Beef in Chile Poblano Sauce

4 pounds (2 kg) tender beef
⅛ onion, chopped
1 clove garlic, chopped
5 ounces (150 g) bacon (chopped)
2 carrots, sliced in strips
3½ ounces (100 g) manchego cheese (or cheddar), chopped
1 potato, peeled and chopped
6 ounces (150 g) ham (sliced thinly)
10 poblano chiles (black ened over fire less than 1 minute, and seeded)
1 tomato
1 clove garlic, cut in half
1 slice onion
3 tablespoons (42 ml) oil
Salt

A cuete is a tender cut of beef from the leg. A rump roast, shoulder roast, or any other large piece of tender beef could be used. A cuete has a shape something like an ice cream roll.

Meat should be cut deeply, circularly, about 1 inch (2 cm) from the edge so that it can be stuffed.

Sauté onion, garlic, bacon, and carrots until they are soft. Add cheese, potato, and ham.

Put the roasted chile *poblanos* in enough water to cover, with the tomato cut in half and the slice of onion. Simmer 10 minutes. Blend.

Stuff the meat with the bacon mixture. Roll and tie in several places and sear in hot oil, turning and browning until it is almost burned.

Add the blended chile mixture to the meat, cover, and simmer about 1½ hours.

Carne de Res con Recado Colorado

Pot Roast with Achiote Paste

Rub meat with the *recado* and let sit a few minutes. Put in boiling, salted water and boil until nearly done, about 1½ hours.

Add tomatoes, onions, and chiles.

Continue cooking until everything is done, and it has cooked down so that it just begins to fry. Stir to keep from sticking.

2 pounds (1 kg) beef (anything that might be used for a pot roast)
1 tablespoon (15 g) *recado de adobo colorado* (see p.119)
4 tomatoes, sliced
2 onions, sliced
3 *jalapeño* chiles, sliced
Salt

Costillas de Res Estilo Guerrero

Boiled Beef Ribs, Guerrero

3 carrots, sliced
8 small potatoes
8 *guajillo* chiles
2 *ancho* chiles
4 tomatoes
1 onion
2 cloves garlic
2 pounds (1 kg) beef ribs
Salt

Boil carrots and potatoes until done. Roast chiles in a *comal* or frying pan until they darken, but don't burn, about 5 minutes. Roast *anchos* a little longer.

Put chiles in water and bring to a boil. Remove from heat and let cool. Blend chiles and strain.

Boil tomatoes, onion, and garlic whole for 15 minutes. Peel skin off of tomatoes. Blend tomatoes, onion, garlic, and chile.

Cut ribs into 2 sections, and boil in enough salted water to cover until done, about ½ hour. The water should be nearly gone when the meat is done.

Add vegetables, chile mixture, and simmer until it is a thick sauce.

Carne de Res Relleno con Jamón y Huevos

Beef Stuffed with Ham and Eggs

Pound the meat unless it is a very tender cut. Marinate in lime juice with salt and pepper to taste for anywhere from a few minutes to several days. Sauté the minced onion and chile in butter. Add the beaten eggs, chopped ham, salt, pepper, and the grated cheese last. Cook until slightly thickened. Spread this mixture on the meat and roll the meat around it. Fasten the meat around the mixture with toothpicks or by sewing. Fry the meat in butter or oil for a few minutes.

Chop and cook the tomatoes until they are a sauce. Add flour to the sauce to thicken. Pour the tomato sauce over the meat. Cover and heat if meat is already tender. If not, simmer until it is, stirring as needed.

1 pound (450 g) beef (a large thin piece, butterflied)
1 lime
Salt and pepper
1 onion, minced
Small, hot chile, minced (to taste)
2 tablespoons (30 g) butter
4 or 5 eggs, beaten
4 or 5 ounces (115-140 g) cooked ham, coarsely chopped
3 or 4 ounces (85-115 g) grated cheese (mozzarella or Monterrey Jack)
8 or 10 tomatoes
1 tablespoon (8.75 g) flour

Tasajo Asado

Dried Beef Broiled over Charcoal

Tasajo is thinly sliced, tender, lean dried beef like that used for carne asada. It is heavily salted and dried in the sun for about a week, similar to salted dried fish. Soak beef for ½ hour and rinse. Dry. Squeeze lime juice (or sour orange, if available) over meat, and broil over charcoal for 2 or 3 minutes. It can also be fried.

Albóndigas de Res

Beef Meatballs

5 canned *chipotle* chiles
2 tomatoes
1 tablespoon (14 ml) oil
Salt
2 eggs
1 pound (450 g) lean
   ground beef
1 tablespoon (15 g) bread
   crumbs
1 tablespoon (6.2 g) finely
   chopped parsley
1 small onion, finely
   chopped

Blend chiles and chopped tomatoes in a *molcajete* or blender. Fry in oil 5 minutes. Add ½ cup (70 ml) water and salt.

Beat the eggs and mix with the meat, breadcrumbs, parsley, and salt. Make little balls about 1 inch (2 cm) in diameter. Should make 30 or more meatballs.

Cook meatballs in pan, covered, about 15 minutes.

Chiles en Nogada

Stuffed Chiles with Walnut Sauce

Steam peppers 5 minutes to remove skins. Cut tops off, but do not discard.

Fry tomatoes, onions, olives, capers, almond, raisins, oregano, and apples with sugar for 20 minutes. Add vinegar while frying.

Chop hard-boiled eggs and mix with everything.

Salt meat and sauté until done, keeping it crumbly.

Mix meat with the tomatoes, onions, etc.

Stuff peppers.

Separate eggs and beat whites until fluffy. Mix in yolks.

Dip chiles in egg and flour, and fry, turning, until light brown. Put on platter so that there are 2 rows of 3 chiles.

Blend walnuts with cream and pour over chiles.

Put parsley over 2 chiles on one end, and pomegranate seeds over the 2 chiles on the other end. The colors will be red, white, and green to represent the Mexican flag. The pomegranate and parsley can be omitted.

6 *poblano* chiles (or bell peppers)
Oil
4 tomatoes, chopped
1 big onion, chopped
12 olives, chopped
3 ounces (85 g) capers
4 ounces (115 g) almonds, ground
4 ounces (115 g) raisins
½ teaspoon (.3 g) oregano
2 apples, peeled and chopped
2 teaspoons (25 g) sugar
1 tablespoon (14 ml) vinegar
3 eggs, hard boiled
Salt and pepper
½ pound (225 g) ground beef
½ pound (225 g) ground pork
3 raw eggs
Flour
1 cup (92 g) shelled walnuts
Cream
2 tablespoons (6.2 g) parsley, chopped
1 pomegranate

Higado de Res con Recado Colorado

Beef Liver with Achiote Paste

4 tomatoes, chopped
1 onion, sliced
4 cloves garlic, roasted,
   peeled, and chopped
1 bell pepper, cut in strips
⅛ teaspoon (.75 g)
   cinnamon
1 clove, ground
Salt
2 tablespoons (30 g)
   recado de adobo colorado
3 tablespoons (42 ml) oil
   or (45 g) lard
1½ pounds (680 g) beef
   liver

Fry the tomatoes, onion, garlic, bell pepper, spices, and the recado in oil for 10 minutes.

Slice the liver into ⅓-inch (1 cm) slices. Salt, and add to the rest of the ingredients. Fry about 5 more minutes, until liver is done.

Riñón de Res con Jerez

Beef Kidney with Sherry

Cut the kidney into pieces, cutting away the fat. Marinate in the vinegar or lime juice a few minutes.

Fry the tomatoes, onion, parsley, salt, and bell pepper in oil for 10 minutes.

Add the kidney and sauté for 8 minutes.

Mix the flour and sherry together until it is smooth. Stir it into the kidney. Sauté for 2 or 3 minutes, stirring until it thickens. Season with salt and pepper.

1½ pounds (680 g) beef kidney
4 tablespoons (56 ml) vinegar or lime juice, or a combination
5 tomatoes, chopped
Onion
3 sprigs parsley, chopped
Salt
1 bell pepper, chopped
2 tablespoons (28 ml) oil
2 tablespoons (17 g) flour
6 ounces (84 ml) sherry
½ teaspoon (3 g) pepper

Lengua Guisada

Beef Tongue Stew

1 to 3 pounds (450 g-1⅓ kg) beef tongue
Salt
3 bay leaves
Oil or butter
1 onion, sliced
2 to 2½ pounds (900 g-1⅓ kg) tomatoes, sliced thin
8 cloves garlic, minced
3 cloves
Peppercorns or ¼ teaspoon (.9 g) black pepper
¼ teaspoon (.25 g) allspice
⅛ teaspoon (.10 g) cinnamon
1 tablespoon (14 ml) vinegar
3 *ancho* chiles
About 1½ cups (75-100 g) mixed prunes (pitted) and raisins
15-20 olives, sliced

Boil tongue in enough water to cover with salt and bay leaves, about 2½ hours. Remove from water and allow to cool. Remove bones, fat, and peel. Slice against grain in about ⅓-inch (1 cm) slices.

Grease a pan and put a layer of tongue on the bottom. Put a layer of onion, tomatoes, and garlic over this. Put another layer of tongue, then the remaining tomatoes, onion, and garlic.

Grind any spice that is not already powdered, and put on top with vinegar.

Devein chiles and put in boiling water. Let sit for about 15 minutes, and blend with prunes and raisins. Add a little water, if necessary.

Pour over top.

Salt and top with olives.

Cover and simmer about 20 minutes. May be necessary to add a little stock that the tongue cooked in to keep it moist and simmering.

Chanfaina Estofada de Tripas de Leche

Tripe Stew

Wash the tripe well. Put the juice from the lime over it, and let marinate for 15 minutes. Put in 2 quarts (2 l) boiling water with salt and 1 clove garlic. Boil gently, covered, for 1 hour. Remove from the water and set aside. Cut in pieces about 1 inch (2 cm) square.

Blend the onion, tomatoes, garlic, chile, and spices, and fry in oil for 10 minutes.

Blend the liver with about 1 cup stock from the tripe, and add to the tomato mixture. Simmer 15 minutes, being careful that it doesn't stick.

Add the tripe, parsley, vinegar, and salt, if necessary, and simmer 5-10 minutes.

1½ pounds (680 g) tripe
Juice of 1 lime
Salt
3 cloves garlic
1 small onion, sliced
½ pound (225 g) tomatoes
2 *ancho* chiles, deveined, seeded, and soaked in hot water
2 cloves, ground
½ teaspoon (1.5 g) black pepper
2 tablespoons oil or lard (28 ml oil, 30 g lard)
½ pound (225 g) beef liver, chopped
2 tablespoons (8 g) chopped parsley
1 tablespoon (14 ml) vinegar

Queso Relleno

Stuffed Cheese

2 balls of Edam cheese
   from Holland
2 pounds (1 kg) ground
   pork
1 pound (450 g) ground
   beef
2 cloves garlic, minced
Salt

Cut a lid in the cheese,
about 3 inches in diame-
ter. Scoop the cheese out
of the ball with a knife or
spoon, whatever seems to
work, until there is a wall
about ½ inch thick.
   Scrape the red paraffin
off the outside.

Sauté the meat with the garlic until meat is browned. Add half
of the following ingredients and simmer 10 minutes.

15 olives, chopped
6 capers (rinsed if salty)
1 heaping tablespoon raisins
10 Italian tomatoes, chopped
1 onion, chopped
2 chiles *xcatic*, chopped
4 eggs, hard boiled, whites finely chopped

Fill the cheese with the meat mixture.

Wrap cheese in a cheese cloth or other light cloth. Steam until
it becomes soft, about 15 minutes. Or put in a baking pan in a
low oven until cheese gets soft, being careful not to let it melt.

Put the other half of the ingredients in a frying pan with the oil
and fry until it is a sauce, about 10 minutes.

For the *kol*, or white sauce:

1 cup (140 g) flour or masa
2 tablespoons (30 g) butter
chicken stock or water
Salt

Melt butter. Mix flour into butter with a little chicken stock.
Stir until it becomes a paste. Continue to add chicken stock,
stirring until it is a thick soup.

To serve, cut a wedge of the cheese and put in a bowl. Spoon
kol over cheese. Spoon tomato sauce over kol. Quite a bit of *kol*
is used, so that the cheese is more or less "swimming" in it.

Lomitos de Valladolid

Pork Stew, Valladolid

Put the meat in boiling, salted water, and allow to cook until done. Try to have the water cook out just as it gets done.

Roast the tomatoes and chile xcatic. Blend the tomatoes and chiles with salt, or grind in a molcajete.

Stir into the meat just as meat is beginning to fry.

Cover and simmer 15 minutes. Serve garnished with chopped egg.

2 pounds (1 kg) boneless pork, cut into bite-size pieces
2 pork kidneys, cut into bite-size pieces
1 pork liver, cut into bite-size pieces
8 tomatoes
1 or 2 chiles *xcatic*
Salt
1 egg, hard boiled

Puerco Royal

Royal Pork

3 pounds (1½ kg) pork loin
Margarine or butter for
   frying + 2 tablespoons
   (30 g) butter
½ pound (225 g) tender
   part of asparagus
½ pound (225 g)
   mushrooms
¾ cup (125 g) tomato sauce
¾ cup (169 ml) heavy cream
Salt
Pepper
1 pound (450 g) small,
waxy   potatoes, peeled
3 tablespoons (26 g) flour

Cut pork into ¾-inch (2 cm) slices, like small steaks. Brown in butter. Put in greased baking dish.

Cut asparagus into 2-inch (5 cm) pieces, using only tender part. Boil asparagus until half done, about 5 minutes.

Slice mushrooms and sauté in the same butter the pork browned in. Put mushrooms over pork. Add asparagus to the baking dish.

Melt 2 tablespoons (30 g) butter in a frying pan. Add 3 cups (675 ml) of the water that the asparagus cooked in, along with the tomato sauce and cream. Add salt and pepper.

Pour sauce into baking dish. Bake in a 425° (220°C) oven for 15 minutes.

Boil potatoes in asparagus water until tender, and serve with pork.

Cochinita Pibil

Pork Baked in Banana Leaves

Salt and baste the pork with *recado colorado*, and let sit for an hour or overnight.

Line a roasting pan with banana leaves, and place the pork on them.

Cover with banana leaves, and bake in a 350° (180° C) oven for about 3 hours or until very tender.

It is often served with *xni-pec*, pickled red onion, and warm tortillas. People often make their own tacos.

4½ **pounds (2 kg) pork for roasting, such as leg or loin**
3½ **ounces (100 g) achiote paste for** *recado colorado*, **dissolved in a little sour orange juice or vinegar**
Salt to taste
Banana leaves

Puerco en Escabeche

Marinated Pork Loin

6 cloves garlic, peeled
2 teaspoons (12.4 g) salt
2 tablespoons (30 g) chopped parsley
1 tablespoon (6.2 g) paprika
½ teaspoon (.3 g) oregano
⅓ cup (94 ml) olive oil
3 pounds (1¼ kg) pork loin
1½ pounds (680 g) small waxy potatoes

Grind the garlic with the salt in a *molcajete* until it is a smooth paste. Grind the parsley into the garlic. Stir in the paprika and oregano. Gradually stir in the olive oil. Cover the pork with this mixture. Cover and refrigerate at least overnight. Turn occasionally.

Boil potatoes in salted water about 10 minutes, let cool and remove jackets.

Put pork in a greased baking dish. Pour marinade over the pork. Put in a 450° (230°C) oven for 10 minutes, then turn to 350° (180°C), and roast about 1½ hours. Add the potatoes in the last 45 minutes.

Puerco con Berenjena y Quimbombó

Pork with Eggplant and Okra

Soak peeled eggplant and okra in salted water for 30 minutes. Dice eggplant, boil 5 minutes in salted water, and drain. Add okra, boil 5 more minutes, and drain. Fry the tomatoes and onion until they form a sauce. Boil the pork in a little water for 1 hour, letting it cook down. Then, add tomato sauce, okra, eggplant, wine, salt, and pepper. Simmer for ½ hour and serve with rice.

1 pound (450 g) eggplant, peeled
½ pound (225 g) okra, sliced
Salt
10 tomatoes
2 onions, chopped
1½ pounds (680 g) pork cut into bite-sized pieces
1 cup (225 ml) red wine

Puerco en Sidra

Pork with Cider

1 pound (450 g) potatoes
4 pounds (2 kg) pork loin
    or leg
10 small cloves garlic
10 prunes with pits
    removed
1 large onion
2 tablespoons (30 g)
    mustard
1 stick butter or
    margarine, melted
1 pint (225 ml) apple cider
1 cup (225 ml) heavy
    cream
1 cup (167 g) catsup
3 tablespoons (42 ml) oil
    to fry apples
4 apples, sliced
Salt

Boil potatoes until tender. Let cool and remove jackets.

Put 10 holes in the meat. Put a prune and garlic clove in each one. Place pork in a greased baking dish. Blend onion and spread over pork. Place pork in a 450° (230°C) pre-heated oven, and reduce the heat to 350° (180°C).

Mix mustard and butter together. Pour over pork when it begins to brown. After 10 minutes, pour ¼ cup apple cider over pork every 15 minutes.

Cook 2 to 2½ hours.

Mix cream and catsup together. Pour about a third of this on pork. Do this two more times at 10 minute intervals. Pour the last of the apple cider over pork just before it is done.

Fry sliced apples in a little oil for 10 minutes, until golden.

Mix some juice from the pork into the potatoes and mash. Keep warm over low heat. Serve pork with apples and potatoes.

Puerco Frito Estilo Guerrero

Fried Pork Ribs Guerrero

Boil ribs with garlic, oregano, and salt in enough water to cover until they are done, about 40 minutes. Adjust water by covering or uncovering pot, as necessary, so that when the ribs are done, the water is almost gone. Squeeze the sour orange into the water, and let cook down until it begins to fry. It should be brown and toasted, beginning to burn.

Serve with refried beans and either of two different sauces.

One sauce:
1 large red onion
4 jalapeño chiles
Salt
Juice of 1 lime

Slice onion thin.

Roast chiles in a frying pan or *comal* 15 minutes. Wrap in a dry paper towel for 5 minutes. Peel skin from chile and chop. Mix all together with salt and lime juice.

The other sauce:
4 tomatoes
10 serrano chiles
Salt

Roast tomatoes in a *comal* or frying pan 15 minutes. Peel. The tomatoes can be wrapped before peeling, but it may not be necessary. Grind chiles in a *molcajete*.

Add the tomatoes and salt, and grind. Add a little water.

This sauce can either be served on the side, or added to the pork with 1 cup water. In the latter case, simmer until it cooks down, about 5 minutes.

2 pounds (1 kg) pork ribs
2 cloves garlic
½ teaspoon (.3 g) oregano
Salt
Sour orange

Cecina con Chiles

Salted Pork with Chiles

Salt
5 *guajillo* chiles
⅛ teaspoon (.08 g)
   cinnamon
2 cloves
¼ teaspoon (.13 g) oregano
1 teaspoon (6.2 g) *hierbas
   de olor* (a mixture of
   thyme, basil and
   marjoram)
2 teaspoons (10 ml)
   vinegar

This recipe is for 1 pound (450 g) of leg or loin of pork, cut thin, like *tasajo*.

Salt the meat (not as if to dry it, but to flavor it) and allow to sit at least two hours.

Remove the stems and seeds from the chiles and heat in a dry pan until dark but not burned. Wrap in a damp cloth, such as a dish towel, for about 10 minutes. When cool, rub off skin. Blend with the other ingredients in a blender or *molcajete*. If necessary, add more vinegar to make a thick sauce. Baste the meat, and allow to sit at least 24 hours. Broil over charcoal until done, about 5 minutes.

Puerco al Horno con Ciruelas Pasas y Crema

Pork with Prune Sauce

Simmer prunes in enough water to cover 15 minutes. Let cool and pit. Blend well with all the other ingredients, and pour over salted roast.

Bake in a 325° (165°C) oven about 2 hours, basting frequently.

Put sweet potatoes in for the last hour. Peel and serve, with sauce over both the meat and potatoes.

1 pound (450 g) prunes
1 *ancho* chile, seeded
2 cloves garlic
1 cup (225 ml) dry white wine
½ cup (108 g) brown sugar
½ teaspoon (1 g) allspice
4 pounds (1¾ kg) pork leg, trimmed of fat
Salt
8 small sweet potatoes

Cochito Horneado

Roast Pork with Chile *Ancho* Sauce

Devein the chiles and fry 5 minutes in oil or lard. Blend with vinegar, salt, and other spices in a blender.

Cut meat into chunks and cover with the chile sauce. Put on a rack in a 350°(180°C) oven for about 30 minutes, until pork is done.

½ pound (225 g) *ancho* chiles
2 tablespoons oil or lard (28 ml oil – 30 g lard)
1 tablespoon (14 ml) vinegar
Salt
4 cloves garlic
¼ teaspoon (1 g) thyme
¼ teaspoon (1.5 g) oregano
½ teaspoon (1.5 g) black pepper
4 pounds (2 kg or 900 g) pork loin

Tiras de Puerco con Cola

Pork Simmered in Cola

1 pound (450 g) lean pork,
    cut in strips about
    ½ inch thick
Salt
Pepper
2 tablespoons (28 ml)
    vinegar, or mixture of
    vinegar and sour orange
2 teaspoons butter or oil
    (10 g butter – 10 ml oil)
1 tablespoon (15 g)
    mustard
1 bell pepper, chopped
6 tomatoes, chopped
1 onion, chopped
1 or 2 *habanero* chiles
8 ounces (224 ml) cola

Marinate meat with salt, pepper, and vinegar for 20 minutes.
Fry meat in oil for 8 minutes.

Put in a pot and mix in 1 teaspoon butter and 1 tablespoon
mustard.

Fry bell pepper, tomatoes, onion, and *habaneros* for 15 minutes
in oil the pork cooked in. Add to pot with meat.

Add cola and liquid that meat marinated in.

Simmer 5 minutes. If the pork is still tough, simmer until tender, adding water if necessary, for about 30 minutes.

Lomo de Puerco al Horno con Cerveza

Pork Loin Baked with Beer

2 teaspoons (4 g) sugar
Salt
1 teaspoon (3.3 g) pepper
2 pounds (1 kg) pork loin
3 tablespoons (42 ml) oil
1 onion, sliced
1 beer

Add sugar, salt, and pepper to meat, and brown in the oil.

Put in a baking dish with the onion and beer, and bake in a
325°(165°C) oven about 45 minutes, until done, basting occasionally with the juice.

Costillas de Puerco a la Parrilla

Grilled Pork Ribs

Boil ribs ½ hour in salted water with 3 cloves garlic and 3 leaves oregano. Remove from water.

To make the *recado*, grind the annatto seeds with a *molcajete*. Add remaining spices and garlic and grind thoroughly, using sour orange juice to make a paste.

Rub the *recado* over the ribs, and grill until done.

For the sauce:

The tomatoes can be roasted over the grill about 10 minutes, over an open fire, or in a *comal* or frying pan. Roast the onion and garlic as in recipe for iguana.

¼ **teaspoon (.5 g) cumin, toasted**
¼ **teaspoon (.15 g) oregano, toasted**
Salt and pepper
3 tablespoons (42 ml) vinegar

Mix the above ingredients with the tomatoes in a blender or *molcajete*. Slice the onions and serve on the side with the garlic and tomato sauce.

There are as many variations for *recado de adobo colorado* as there are for meatloaf. But regardless of anything to the contrary printed or said, there is no doubt in my mind that the flavor of achiote is important. It is not just for coloring. There is no substitute.

2 pounds (1 kg) pork ribs
3 cloves garlic
1½ (1 g) teaspoons oregano

For the *recado de adobo colorado*:

1 tablespoon (15 g) annatto seeds
1 teaspoon (3.3 g) pepper
1 teaspoon (2 g) cumin
2 cloves
1 ball of allspice
5 cloves garlic
Sour orange
10 Italian plum tomatoes
10 small onions
½ head garlic

Puerco Entomatado

Pork Stew with Tomato Sauce

2 pounds (1 kg) boneless
   pork, chopped
1 onion, chopped
1 bell pepper, chopped
10 tomatoes, chopped
2 *habanero* chiles, chopped
Salt

Boil pork in enough salted water to nearly cover for about 30 minutes. Uncover, if necessary, to allow water to cook down. Add the rest of the ingredients and cook until they have cooked down to a sauce and the pork is done.

Frijol con Puerco

Pork with Black Beans

Boil beans with epazote until they begin to get soft. You can add pork bones to boil with the beans. Add the pork and half the onion. Cook until beans and pork are done, about 2 hours. Add salt toward the end. Salt toughens beans if added early.

Cook rice with water from beans. It's called *arroz negro* (black rice).

Roast the tomatoes and chiles in a dry *comal* or frying pan, or over an open flame.

Blend the tomatoes, or grind with a *molcajete*. Serve on the side. Grind the chiles with a little water or sour orange. Serve on the side. People who serve it this way put a small amount of the liquid on tortillas.

Mix the cilantro, radishes, and half the onion and serve on the side. If this had sour orange in it, it would be *salpicón*. Without it it is merely a condiment. Some people mix the *habanero* with this.

The pork, rice, and avocado are served on a plate. The beans and liquid in which they cooked are served in a bowl.

1 pound (450 g) dried black beans
Epazote
½ pound (225 g) ribs (for flavor)
1 pound (450 g) boneless pork, cut into chunks
1 large onion, chopped
Salt
1 cup (192 g) rice
5 tomatoes
2 *habanero* chiles, chopped
Cilantro, chopped
About 10 radishes, coarsely chopped
Avocado
Lime

Pezuñas con Garbanzos

Pigs Feet with Garbanzos

2 pounds (1 kg) pigs feet
1 teaspoon (.6 g) oregano
Salt and pepper
1 onion, sliced
2 chiles *xcatic*
2 tablespoons (28 ml)
  vinegar
2 cups (364 g) cooked
  garbanzos, drained
1 large *chayote*, sliced
3 carrots, peeled and
  sliced

Put pigs feet in 1 quart (1 l) water. Add the spices, onion, chiles, and vinegar. Boil 1½ hours, or until pig feet are nearly done. Add the garbanzos and sliced vegetables and continue cooking until done. Add water as necessary.

Potaje

Pork, Ham and Sausage Stew

Potaje is a natural thing to think of along with *puchero*. The names are about as similar as the dishes. Potaje can be made with *frijol vaya* (kidney beans), white beans, lentils, or garbanzos. Irma said it is best with white beans.

Cook beans with epazote in unsalted water until nearly done. Add salt.

Fry *salchichas*, bacon, ham, and chorizo in olive oil for 5 minutes. Add onion, tomatoes, and bell pepper, and fry for 10 minutes. Add garlic, cloves, and paprika, and fry for 5 minutes.

Add carrots, cabbage, potatoes, and squash to beans.

Add the tomato and meat mixture to beans and cook for 30 minutes. Serve with rice on the side.

1 pound (450 g) white beans
Sprig epazote
Salt
3 tablespoons (42 ml) olive oil
6 ounces (180 g) *salchichas* (if unavailable, hot dogs can be used)
2 ounces (60 g) bacon, preferably smoked
¼ pound (115 g) ham, cut into chunks
1½ pounds (680 g) pork, cut into chunks
10 inch (25 cm) chorizo
Olive oil
1 onion, chopped
10 Italian plum tomatoes, chopped
2 bell peppers, chopped
4 cloves garlic, minced
3 cloves, ground
3 tablespoons (10 g) paprika
4 carrots, sliced
⅓ head cabbage, sliced
4 potatoes, peeled and chopped
2 medium squash, coarsely chopped
Rice

Puchero con Tres Carnes

Chicken, Pork and Beef Stew

3 cloves garlic, sliced
4 leaves oregano
½ teaspoon (1.5 g) pepper
¼ teaspoon (.5 g) cumin
¼ teaspoon (.18 g) cilantro
  (coriander) seeds,
  crushed
1 chicken
1 pound (450 g) pork, cut
  into pieces roughly ¾
  inch square
1 pound (450 g) beef, cut
  into similar pieces
8 inches (20 cm) of
  chorizo (optional)
2 cups (500 g) garbanzos
3 small or one large
  squash
2 *chayotes*
1 *plátano macho* (cooking
  banana)
3 carrots
1 head garlic
4 small onions, or one big
  one cut into quarters
½ small cabbage, sliced
  thin (optional)
2 tablespoons (30 g)
  uncooked rice
2 or 3 ounces (60-85 g) of
  fideos, or vermicelli
  broken into pieces
  (optional)
Salt

Put the 3 cloves garlic and spices in enough salted water to cover meat. Bring to a boil. Add the chicken, pork, and beef, and allow to boil covered for about ½ hour.

Add the pre-cooked garbanzos and the other vegetables, including the roasted garlic and onion. If using cabbage, add it a few minutes later, along with the rice. Add the *fideos* last. To have everything cooked evenly, it may be necessary to remove some items while the rest continues to boil.

Served on the side:

Radishes, chopped
Cilantro, chopped
Onion, chopped
Sour orange

All mixed together and served in a bowl.

Higado de Puerco con Mole Colorado

Pork Liver with Mole Colorado

Fry the garlic, onion, and bell pepper in the oil for about 5 minutes. Slice the liver into pieces about ⅓ inch (1 cm) wide, and add to pan. Fry about 2 minutes on each side.

For the Mole Colorado:

Prepare the chiles as in *a la diabla* sauce. Prepare the tomatoes, onion, and garlic as for iguana sauce.

Toast the sesame seeds in a dry pan, but do not burn. Do the same with the peanuts.

Grind the peppercorns, cloves, and cinnamon (if a stick is used) in a *molcajete,* along with the nuts. Blend everything together in a blender or *molcajete,* and fry in a little oil for about 10 minutes.

Mix with the liver and sauté about 10 minutes.

There should be more than enough sauce for the liver. The sauce is also good on chicken, and in the following recipe for pozole.

1 clove garlic
1 onion, thinly sliced
1 bell pepper
3 tablespoons butter or oil (45 g butter - 42 ml oil)
Salt
1½ pounds (680 g) pork liver (or beef liver)

MOLE COLORADO
½ pound (225 g) chile *ancho*
¼ pound (115 g) red chile *pasilla*
1 pound (450 g) of tomatoes
1 onion
1 head garlic
6 peppercorns
3 cloves
1 small stick cinnamon (about ⅛ teaspoon (.15 g), ground)
2 tablespoons (18 g) sesame seeds
1½ ounces (45 g) almonds
1½ ounces (45 g) raw peanuts without skins
1½ ounces (45 g) pecans
1 tablespoon (1.2 g) oregano

Pozole con Mole

Pozole with Mole

1 pound (450 g) pork head (or any other part with bones)
1 pound (450 g) pigs feet
1 onion, chopped
3 cloves garlic, chopped
2 15-ounce (425 g) cans hominy, drained
1½ quarts (1½ l) water
Salt

Cut the pork into ½ to 1-inch (1½-2½ cm) square chunks. Boil with the garlic, onion, and feet, about 1 hour, until nearly done. Add hominy during the last 20 minutes.

Serve with heated *mole colorado* on the side, to spoon into the soup.

Albóndigas de Puerco

Pork Meatballs

Prepare chiles as in recipe for *a la diabla* sauce.

Grind tomatoes with garlic and spices, and fry in oil 5 minutes. Take 1 tablespoon (15 g) to mix with the meat. Put the rest in 1 quart (1 l) boiling, salted water with chiles.

Beat eggs. Mix with salt, meat, parsley, breadcrumbs, and onion. Brown in oil for 5 minutes, turning. Put in boiling tomato mixture and simmer uncovered for 20 minutes.

Albóndiga is not a soup, but there should be enough liquid to put on the rice that commonly accompanies it.

2 *pasilla* chiles
2 tomatoes
2 cloves garlic
2 cloves
⅛ teaspoon (.15 g) cinnamon (or piece of stick that will make this much when ground)
2 tablespoons (28 ml) oil
3 eggs
Salt
1 pound (450 g) ground pork
1 tablespoon (6.2 g) finely chopped parsley
1 tablespoon (.5 g) breadcrumbs
1 onion, finely chopped

Chicharrón con Ancho Chile

Cracklings with Chile Ancho

3 *ancho* chiles
½ onion, chopped
1 slice bacon
6 tomatoes, chopped
½ pound (225 g) cracklings
    with meat, broken in
    pieces
2 cups (450 g) cooked
    lentils
Salt
Oil for frying

Seed chiles and bring to a boil. Let soak until cool.

Fry onion with bacon until soft. Add tomatoes and chiles and fry for 5 minutes. Add cracklings and about 1 cup (140 ml) of the water the chiles were in. Simmer for 25 minutes. Add water if necessary. Stir in lentils at the end to warm.

Served with rice.

Carne de Res Molido con Chilmole

Ground Meat with Blackened Chile Sauce

Fry tomatoes and onion in oil for 5 minutes.

Put chilmole in a pan with a little vinegar and water. Heat, stir, and smash with a spoon, until it's a thick liquid. Add to meat. (To make *chilmole* from scratch, see recipe for *pavo en relleno negro*. Most people buy it already prepared.)

Fry meat with tomato mixture until nearly done, stirring. Stir beans into meat, and continue cooking until meat is done.

This was served with rice, boiled squash, and white bread with margarine on the side.

2 tablespoons (28 ml) oil
4 tomatoes
2 onions
3½ ounces (100 g box) *chilmole*
Vinegar
1 pound (450 g) ground beef
1 pound (450 g) ground pork
½ pound (225 g) finely chopped ham
16 ounces (450 g) cooked black beans
1 cup (160 g) crushed cracker crumbs
3 eggs, hard boiled
⅛ teaspoon (.75 g) cinnamon
Salt

Asado de Cerdo

Roast Pork Leg

10 tomatoes
6 *jalapeño* chiles
4 pound (2 kg) pork leg
Salt
Lettuce and radishes for
　garnish

Blend tomatoes and chiles, seeds and all. Boil in 2 cups water for 20 minutes.

Salt pork. Pour sauce over it, and bake in a 325° (165°C) oven 2 hours, basting occasionally.

Conejo con Mezcal

Rabbit with Mezcal

Salt the rabbit and sprinkle with sage. Fry in ¼ inch (1 cm) very hot oil, turning until browned.

Add all the other ingredients. Cover and simmer until done, about 45 minutes, adding a little water, if necessary.

1 rabbit, cut into pieces
Heart and liver, finely chopped (chicken can be substituted)
¼ teaspoon (.5 g) sage
½ cup (112 ml) olive oil
Oil
Greens of 3 onions, finely sliced
3 *jalapeños,* seeded and chopped
2 tablespoons (12.5 g) finely chopped parsley
1 cup (140 g) mezcal
Salt

Hu en Chile Guajillo

Iguana in *Guajillo* Chile Sauce

1 or 2 iguanas
1 quart (1 l) water
3 ounces (100 g) chile
   guajillo
7 ounces (200 g) tomatoes
1 onion
½ head garlic
½ tablespoon (2 g)
   oregano
1 cinnamon stick
2 sprigs of thyme
3 tablespoons (44 ml) oil

Scorch the iguana over a fire until it is black. Pull the skin off. Slit down the stomach and remove the intestines. Wash and put it in a pot of the boiling water, salt, 2 or 3 cloves of garlic, and the onion. Simmer until done, about 40 minutes. Remove the iguana from the liquid, remove another layer of skin, and cut it into several pieces.

Remove the chile stems and seeds and prepare them as for a la diabla sauce. Roast the tomatoes, garlic, and onion in a comal or frying pan until they are black. The tomato takes 20 minutes to ½ hour. The onion and garlic can be done over an open fire. The onion takes 5 to 10 minutes on each side. The garlic blackens in 10 to 15 minutes. Do not dust off the blackened part. Grind these, along with the spices and drained chiles either in a blender or with a molcajete. Strain and fry in 3 tablespoons (44 ml) oil for about 10 minutes. Mix with the liquid the iguana cooked in, and add iguana. Heat and serve with rice and beans.

Chicken can be substituted for iguana in this dish. It is not difficult to prepare, and the taste could make you feel like a real southern Mexican chef, even if you are not.

Cascabela Salteada

Gilda's Recipe for Rattlesnake Sauté

Dip snake in milk, then flour. Sauté in oil, turning until pale golden all over.

If Gilda lived in southern Mexico, she would probably marinate the snake in lime juice.

This is quite a delicacy.

1 rattlesnake, skinned, cleaned, and cut into 1 inch pieces
Milk
Salted flour
Oil, about ⅓ inch (1 cm) deep
Pepper

 HUHÍ

Maketch is the Maya word for a type of tan beetle that lives on the rainforest floor in the Yucatán. Trapped and adorned with saddles of sequins and a gold-colored chain and safety pin, these beetles are sold in the market in Mérida, along with a piece of wood from their natural habitat and a small container to keep them in. Pinned to garments, the bugs become living jewelry.

Maketches live from six months to a year, depending on how old they are when captured. While in captivity, they drink from the wood, which must be watered every few days. They do not seem to eat. Nor do they have functioning reproductive systems. Left to roam around a terrarium or a box, they are entertaining to watch: they walk about aimlessly, changing direction for no apparent reason, climbing over one another and toppling off, and generally acting like comics in a silent slapstick show. Some people assume that the decorated beetles are battery-operated devices made in Japan; others, especially animal activists, might be infuriated at the way they are treated. It seems to me that they can be regarded with as much respect as fish in an aquarium.

Years ago, in an effort to return from the Yucatán with Christmas presents, I smuggled twelve *maketches* into the United States under my shirt. The customs official, taking his good time rooting through my bag, never noticed my shirt bunching up as the bugs crawled about beneath it. All the while, not knowing what becomes of convicted beetle smugglers, I was extremely nervous.

Living in Mérida, I developed a type of beetle mania of a different sort: I wanted some unadorned ones to keep in a box and look at when there was nothing better to do. Returning to the market, I was able to find my way not only to beetles but to some savory recipes. The *maketch*-monger, who sold only adorned bugs, refused to tell me where they came from; but a young man selling dresses in the next stall, having overheard our conversation, waved me over to come speak with him. We communicated in broken Spanish, his Maya, and my English. He explained that the *maketch* designer and distributor was a man named Ramón Pech, who lived in the pueblo of Huhí. He explained that as a child he used to catch *maketches* for Pech. Then he told me how to get to Pech's house and added that I should say Fausto sent me. The *maketch* monger, realizing that his secret was lost, no longer wanted to be left out. He came over to give me directions to Huhí.

In Quest of *Maketches*

The next day, Gilda, my ex-wife, accompanied me to Huhí. The pueblo, about forty miles southeast of Mérida, is accessible only by paved back roads. The winding road leading to Huhí suddenly narrows as one approaches town. On the outside of a turn much sharper than the others, I noticed a huge rock about ten feet from the road. The rock was rather pretty because it was covered not only by the usual white fecal matter from buzzards but by colorful streaks of automotive paint—signs from some of the inhabitants of the region.

I later learned that the most recent streak came from the Huhí town mechanic's car. He showed me the vehicle in his backyard; a front fender and one side were crushed in. Mixed with the remorse in his voice was a hint of excitement, as though he was ever so slightly proud of the mishap. I also learned that Huhíites buy Sol beer in cartons of twenty from the El Cenote cantina. This practice may be responsible for some of the colors that complement the white on the rock outside of town.

After pulling into Huhí, Gilda and I saw, standing in front of the house I thought must be Pech's, a woman weighing more than 200 pounds. She was indeed Señora Pech and very friendly as well. She told us that her husband was in Mérida. She had expected him to return on the previous bus, but now it would be another hour and a half before his arrival.

To pass the time, Gilda and I decided to visit some of the nearby pueblos, but a few miles outside of Huhí we saw an injured rattlesnake on the road. Someone had run over it. So we parked at the side of the road and got out of the truck. During our twenty-four year haitus, Gilda had learned how to make belts and other items out of leather and rattleskin. She once gave a belt to Hank Williams Jr. and said that it pleased him. On the road to Huhí, she decided to go back into business. She held the snake's head down with a stick while I cut it off with my knife. I trusted her as I always had, and she did not let go of the rattler's head until it was completely severed.

Because my knife was too dull for Gilda to work with, we returned to Huhí and stopped at the El Cenote to find a sharper one. The borrowed knife was perfect. Gilda set about cleaning and skinning the snake in front of the cantina.

Within minutes, dogs and people had gathered to watch the gringa clean her rattlesnake. They undoubtedly came for the same reason, for the dogs would have nothing to do with the snake's intestines—they just sat and watched. Even the proprietor watched for a while. He eventually disappeared inside, though, for the activity had attracted several new customers.

Cleaning a rattlesnake in public is a good way to meet people. A couple of guys in the crowd proudly began speaking English to us. They were celebrating the last day of their vacation. The next morning they would be returning to Los Angeles to lay carpets in high-rise buildings. Before finding work in Los Angeles, they, too, had been *maketch* hunters for Señor Pech. I gathered that his enterprise was an integral part of the child economy of Huhí, somewhat akin to paper routes in the United States.

Around 3:50 PM, the owner of the El Cenote stepped outside again, obviously anxious. Cantinas in the pueblos are supposed to close at four o'clock, he said, and he was having a hard time shutting down. To speed things up, he brought out plastic bags for the snake's skin, meat, and intestines. We filled the bags appropriately, whereupon he took his knife and the bag of intestines inside and closed the door.

Climbing into the truck with the two remaining plastic bags, Gilda talked about dipping the cut-up rattlesnake in milk and flour and sautéeing it in butter—which she did several days later, much to the delight of her dinner guests. We heard a bus come into town, so it was time to return to the Peches' house. As soon as we pulled up, the señora appeared and motioned to us to come in. Ramón, a thin man in his early forties and about five feet, four inches tall, smiled inquisitively while shaking my hand.

"What a couple!" I thought. I told him I wanted to buy some *maketches*.

"Ah, *maketches*," he said, the inquisitive part of his smile disappearing.

He hurried toward the kitchen, bidding me to follow. While we talked about *maketches,* he zipped around the room as though wired on stimulants. I came to learn that he always acted this way.

The house was teeming with so much commotion that it had a bus station aura about it—which may or may not be related to the fact that the bus stops a few feet from the front door. The four Pech children, neighborhood kids, and an occasional adult milled about, coming or going with seeming randomness. I did notice Señora Pech handing money to a couple of kids and taking a shoe box from them—bugs, no doubt. I told Ramón I wanted thirty beetles, unadorned. He did not have that many on hand, he said. He had just taken his last batch to Mérida but would deliver thirty beetles at one o'clock the next afternoon.

Returning to the truck, I could barely wait to tell Gilda something that had sprung up from the recesses of my mind the moment I observed this bug seller's size and behavior. "Pech," I told her, "is Maya for 'tick.' "

The next day, Gilda and I began speculating about what time Pech would show up, if at all—two o'clock? four o'clock? But at 12:50 PM there was a knock at the door. "Tick's here already!" I opened the door, and there he was, with newly shined shoes, a nice *guayabera* shirt, and a leather briefcase. A cellular phone was all that was missing. He stepped inside. Opening his briefcase, he took out a coffee can with holes punched in the sides and poured thirty *maketches* onto the nearest table, along with a lot of wood.

We invited him to sit down and offered him a beer. He accepted and in the course of our conversation invited us to his house for dinner the following Sunday. I mentioned that I had had *pavo en relleno negro* (turkey stuffed with ground pork in blackened chile sauce) (p. 161) at Tucho's in Mérida and thought it was very good. He said that is what we would have on Sunday. Then he stood, shook our hands, and slowly backed up toward the door before turning and darting off like the March Hare.

Family-style a la Pech or Informal Dining at the Pech's

When we arrived on Sunday, we were greeted by not only the Pech children but a pack of others. Papa was not there, they told us, and Mama was asleep in a hammock stretched across the front room. She had already eaten. Where was Papa? *Quién sabe.*

We sat at the table with several of the children while sixteen-year-old Louisa, the oldest of the Tick kids, served us. A grandmother wandered in and sat at the table to watch the gringos eat. Then Ramón came in with another man, shook our hands, and introduced us to his companion, the mayor of Huhí—whom we had met several days before, in front of the El Cenote. They sat down for a quick beer and left. The señora came in, said hello, picked some meat from the pot on the stove, wrapped it in a couple of tortillas, and sauntered out back to wash clothes. A neighbor came in with a small pot, spooned some food into it, and left. A young woman came in and sat at the table to chat and pick at the food. I soon learned that every time food was served at the Peches, it was as though someone had stood at the front door and hollered, "Sooey!"

The mother returned from the backyard wiping her wet hands on an apron. She picked some more meat from the pot and sat by the tortillas. I asked her how to make *pavo en relleno negro* (which was not what had been served). In response, Louisa started yelling instructions to me while pantomiming the motions, her hands flailing as she walked back and forth between the stove and me. Finally, her mother said that if we came the following Sunday, she would make it and we could watch. The children all beamed; they were crazy about Gilda and looked forward to seeing her again.

The mother gave me a list of ingredients to bring from Mérida. Starting from scratch, she explained, is better than using the ready-made *chilmole* paste. She would, of course, provide the turkey, and she would get the chiles nearby because the locally grown ones were best. I gave her the money she said they would cost, surprised at how much it was. I learned that a lot of chiles are used in this dish.

Louisa told me that by watching her mother, she had learned to make everything her mother made and that she had learned to cook by watching her mother. The grandmother smiled and nodded. Jotting down recipes is not a customary practice in the pueblos, for it is mostly the young people who have learned to write.

Auri, the youngest in the family—a pretty girl of eight with a face reminiscent of the ancient Maya—put a record on the record player. Then she placed a beer bottle filled with water on her head and, together with a couple of neighborhood girls, proceeded to entertain Gilda with folk dancing. I, meanwhile, wrote in my notebook while Louisa told me how to make what we had just eaten: *carne de res con tomate* (strips of beef with tomato) (p. 95), *ensalada de calabazas* (squash salad) (p. 69), *frijoles negros* (village-style black beans) (p. 76), and *xni-pec* (tomato and chile relish) (pg. 21).

Unable to stop, Louisa continued with recipes for other beef dishes, among them *carne de res en escabeche* (beef with pickled red onion) (p. 96), *carne de res relleno con jamón y huevo* (beef stuffed with ham and eggs) (p. 101), *carne de res con yema* (beef with egg yolk) (p. 97), and *carne de res con recado colorado* (beef pot roast with achiote) (p. 99). She was so enthusiastic that she reminded me of a drama student performing a portion of her repertoire at the command of the teacher.

Foul Boil

When we parked in front of the Pech's house a week later, a large pack of children gathered around us. As we emerged from the truck with the ingredients for dinner, several kids latched onto Gilda's arms and legs, talking as fast as they could in Spanish; Gilda responded in English. Others followed us into the open house, the smallest ones showing off by running around and rolling on the floor. When Señora Pech came to take the ingredients and give Gilda a hug, the children holding onto her scattered like minnows.

Ramón followed with a beer for each of us and an offer to sit on his finest furniture. He was excited. In fifteen minutes he was to be at the baseball field outside of town to announce game four of the playoffs between the Huhí Buitres (Buzzards) and the Xocchal Leones (Lions). We decided that I would go to the game while Gilda stayed at the house to watch the making of *pavo en relleno negro* from scratch. Little did we know that "from scratch" included killing the turkey.

Ramón and I set off in my truck. The road was crowded with people walking the mile or so to the Huhí baseball field. Every few seconds Ramón would wave at someone and ask me to stop so that the person could jump in the back of the truck. By the time we got to the field, my pickup had people hanging all over it, like children on Gilda.

It was a pretty good baseball field—smooth grass, lime baselines, a concrete home-run fence. The only noticeable flaw was a small pyramid in deep right field. I do not think it was an ancient ruin; more likely, dirt had been placed around a rock that was too big to move. Although a large tree provided shade for most of the home-team bleachers and a booth under the tree provided shelter for the announcer, Tick chose to set up his portable loud speaker system at the end of the bleachers, just beyond the shady area. Our seats were closer to home plate and within two arms' reach of the beer monger on the ground below.

I picked the Leones to win. Not only had they already won two of the three playoff games, but they had matching uniforms. Only four or five of the Huhí players had a large red buzzard on the front of their shirts. Some even wore jeans.

Soon after we were seated, the woman on my right began talking to me. She proudly pointed out her daughter who had been dubbed Queen of Izamal at the festival the night before. Festivals occur regularly in Yucatán towns in the summer. I asked the woman if she wanted a beer, and she said, "No thanks, too much fiesta last night." Then she clenched her fist, stuck out her thumb and little finger, put her thumb to her mouth, and threw her head back—executing the Mexican national gesture for drinking alcohol.

Ramón was a good announcer. From the start he kept the baseball talk constant, even between innings. After the top of the third, he began to plug beer. As the innings progressed, Ramón's advertising increased, and each time he would check on me, then a few of his very good *amigos* who had gathered to stand in the sun, before passing around enough beers for each of us. Somewhere in the fifth inning, he said into the microphone: "Sol and Superior beer—Yucatán's best. There is nothing better than a cold beer on a hot day like this." It was getting hard not to laugh at the scene.

In the bottom of the seventh, a Buzzard hit three fouls in a row into an adjoining *henequen* field. The game was stopped while children scampered into the field to find the balls. Ramón took advantage of this break to do some serious advertising, and all his friends were rewarded, even if the bottles already in their hands were full.

If Tick was good to begin with, by the late innings he was great. His vivacity, never flagging, had gained momentum. By the eighth inning he had taken to advertising between batters. By the ninth he was quite full of Sol. With a bottle of beer in one hand and the microphone in the other, he was like the Wizard of Oz but with no need to hide behind a curtain.

Huhí's uniforms bespoke their ability, and they lost a well-played game 1 to 0. Old Tick was really vigorous after the game, almost ranting. He was not upset that Huhí had lost; rather, he was excited that it had been a good game and, more importantly, that he had been a good announcer. Had he not kept the crowd tranquil? Did I see one fight, one act of violence? he wanted to know. *"No problemas!"* he roared, leaving me no time to answer his questions.

The ride home was filled with Tick's jubilant, if incoherent, commentary—*"No problemas! Tranquilo!* You are my good *amigo"*—followed by an impressive array of hand signs. Back home, he escorted me to the kitchen where everyone had congregated and commended himself to his family for the tranquil atmosphere at the game. He looked at me as if to garner support on this matter. Then he left the house.

Gilda and I sat down to dine with Louisa, Auri, and a couple of neighbors, while Señora Pech stood around the kitchen nibbling. Gilda said the señora had been picking at the turkey ever since it had become tender enough to chew. The *pavo en relleno negro,* rice, tortillas, *calabazas,* black beans, and *salsa verde* were already on the table, so we helped ourselves to what turned out to be a delicious meal. We were joined by Ramón and two friends—the mayor, whom we had already met twice, and a pitcher for the

Buzzards. They stayed just long enough to eat before shaking our hands and excusing themselves.

Louisa then handed a stack of papers to Gilda. On them were instructions for each of the dishes we were served as well as recipes for *pollo pibil* (chicken with achiote baked in banana leaves) (p. 153), its pork counterpart *cochinita pibil* (p. 111), *pollo en escabeche* (chicken in onion and vinegar) (p. 152), and *pollo asado con sopa de fideo* (chicken with vermicelli, grilled with achiote) (p. 154).

The señora gave Gilda and me the beers that were left in the refrigerator, ensuring that her husband would have nothing to fall back on when he came home.

"Make that one for the road a Sol," she told us. So we did.

There is nothing like a Sol or Superior on a balmy night while driving with the windows down singing, "I told the witch doctor I was in love with you . . . and then the witch doctor, he told me what to do . . . he said that oo-ee-oo-ah-ah . . . ."

AVES de CORRAL

Reading these recipes will help the cook to understand the versatility and adaptability of Yucatán cooking. Many methods of preparation can be used for more than one kind of meat.

Pollo Estragón en Salsa de Crema

Tarragon Chicken in Cream Sauce

1 chicken
3 cups (675 ml) stock
1 teaspoon (.6 g) thyme
1 bay leaf
2 teaspoons (4 g) tarragon
12 mushrooms, trimmed
   and sliced
1½ cups (337 ml) dry white
   wine
3 tablespoons (45 g)
   butter
Salt
Pepper
1 tablespoon (15 g) flour
½ cup (112 ml)
   heavy cream

Disjoint chicken. Boil neck and giblets to make 3 cups (675 ml) stock.

Mix thyme, bay leaf, tarragon, mushrooms, and wine into stock. Add chicken and cook until tender, about 40 minutes.

Melt butter and mix with flour and cream. Cook over low heat until thickened, about 5–7 minutes.

Put sauce on chicken and serve.

Pollo Alberto

Chicken with Pineapple and Orange Juice

Boil chicken 20 minutes with oregano, mint, pepper, bay leaves, and salt.

Fry onions and chile in oil until onions are soft.

Add chicken. Set aside the water used to cook the chicken.

Add salt, pepper, and garlic.

Cover and simmer 20 minutes. If it becomes too dry, add a little of the water used to cook the chicken.

Serve with rice.

1 chicken, quartered
1 teaspoon (.5 g) oregano
1 teaspoon (3.3 g)
  chopped mint leaves
Pepper
2 bay leaves
Salt
Oil
2 onions
Chile *xcatic*
2 cloves garlic, minced
1 can pineapple, drained
1 cup (225 ml)
  orange juice

Pollo con Piña

Chicken with Pineapple

1 large pineapple
1 onion, chopped
2 cloves garlic, minced
½ cup (112 ml) oil
1 chicken, quartered
1 cup (225 ml) tomato
   sauce
1 bay leaf
Salt
½ teaspoon (1.5 g) pepper
1 bell pepper, cut in strips
¼ teaspoon (1.5 g)
   monosodium glutamate
   (optional)
2 *serrano* chiles, cut into
   strips

Cut the pineapple meat into ½ inch (1½ cm) pieces.

Sauté onion and garlic in oil until onion becomes soft.

Add chicken and sauté until golden.

Add tomato sauce, bay leaf, salt, and pepper. Simmer covered for 15 to 20 minutes.

Add pineapple, peppers, and monosodium glutamate (optional). Cover and simmer 10 more minutes. Do not allow to dry out.

Serve with rice.

Piña Rellena con Pollo

Pineapple Stuffed with Chicken

Cut chicken into ½ inch (1½ cm) cubes.

Slice tops off of pineapples and scoop out the meat. Slice a little off the bottom so the pineapple will stand.

Put onion, celery, pineapple, green pepper, and carrot in a pan. Add vinegar, water, and sugar and simmer covered for 30 minutes.

Add tomato sauce, salt, pepper, and ginger.

Mix cornstarch with a little water and add to pan, stirring until it thickens.

Melt butter in a frying pan. Add the chicken and sauté for 3 or 4 minutes without browning.

Add sauce to chicken and simmer for 5 minutes.

Pour into pineapple and replace pineapple tops.

Serve with rice.

A small papaya cut in half can be substituted for the pineapple.

1 chicken
2 pineapples
1 small onion, chopped
1 stalk celery, chopped
½ bell pepper, chopped
1 carrot, sliced thin
2 teaspoons (10 ml) vinegar
2 teaspoons (10 g) sugar
2 teaspoons (10 ml) tomato sauce
Salt
Pepper
½ teaspoon (1 g) ginger
1 teaspoon (3.3 g) cornstarch
1 tablespoon (15 g) butter or margarine
1 cup (225 ml) water

Pollo al Horno con Cebolla Cambray

Baked Chicken with Cambray Onions

About ½ teaspoon (1.5 g)
  each: thyme, marjoram,
  nutmeg, pepper, sage
1 tablespoon (2 g)
  powdered chicken
  bouillon (or 1 cube,
  dissolved and poured
  over chicken before
  putting in oven)
Flour
1 chicken
1 stick butter or
  margarine
15–20 cambray onions,
  green removed
6 ounces (168 ml) white
  wine
Oil
½ pound (225 g)
  mushrooms, or 1 can
1 pound (450 g) carrots
2 tablespoons (30 g)
  butter
1½ tablespoons (21 ml)
  honey
3 tablespoons (10 g)
  chopped mint
Rice

A friend of Alberto's in Mexico City, a German woman, had been a cook for the former Queen Mary when she was in France. This is one of the dishes she used to prepare for her.

Mix spices with powdered chicken bouillon and flour. Put in a bag. Put chicken in bag and shake thoroughly.

Place the chicken in a greased baking dish. Put the stick of butter on top and the onions around it. Add the wine. Bake in a 350° (180°C) oven for 1 hour.

For the gravy, sauté the mushrooms in a small amount of oil until soft. Add juice from the casserole. Slowly add flour and water mixed together, stirring until it thickens to gravy.

Peel the carrots and slice fairly thin.

Boil with very little water, removing cover so that water has boiled out after 20 minutes.

Add 2 tablespoons (30 g) butter, honey, and mint and simmer for 5 minutes.

Serve chicken and onions on a plate with rice and carrots. Spoon gravy over chicken and rice.

Budín Azteca

Chicken and Cuitlacoche Casserole

Boil chicken with salt, carrot, onion, and garlic for about 45 minutes.

Sauté the squash flowers, without stems, in 1 tablespoon (14 ml) oil for 1 minute on each side. They will become soft and limp.

Cut off the cuitlacoche and corn with a sharp knife down to the cob. Do the same with the other ears. Sauté the corn in the rest of the oil for about 8 minutes.

Roast the chiles over an open fire or a gas burner for 3-5 minutes, turning until blistered more or less all over. Wrap them in a dampened dish towel for 10 minutes. This makes them easier to peel. You can scrape the peel off with your fingernail. You might be able to do this without waiting, but you need not be meticulous in peeling them. Remove the seeds and veins.

Shred the cooled chicken with fingers or a fork.

Dip each tortilla in the water used to cook the chicken, and cover the bottom of a greased baking dish. Some people dip the chicken in tomato sauce, but others like it better without. Put a layer of shredded chicken, distribute some squash flowers, corn, and *cuitlacoche*. Repeat until ingredients are gone. It's a good idea to have a can of cuitlacoche on hand, should you not have enough.

Put the grated cheese on top.

Blend chiles with ¼ cup (56 ml) chicken stock and ¼ cup (56 ml) cream in a blender. Pour over top, and bake at 350° (180°C) for about 30 minutes.

1 large chicken
Salt
1 carrot
1 onion
1 clove garlic
Squash flowers, 10 or more (it's hard to have too many)
3 tablespoons (42 ml) oil
2–3 large ears of corn with *cuitlacoche*
2 ears of corn (1½ frozen can be substituted, with some loss of flavor)
3 to 4 *poblano* chiles
About 20 corn tortillas, or 1 pound (450 g)
½ pound (225 g) Chihuahua cheese (or Oaxacan cheese–mild cheddar or Monterrey Jack can be used)
¼ cup (56 ml) cream
1 can tomato sauce (optional)

 Alcaparrado

Capered Chicken

1 chicken
2 ounces (60 g) squash
   seeds, or pumpkin seeds
4 cloves
4 peppercorns
1 small stick of cinnamon
5 threads of saffron
¼ tablespoon (1 g) oregano
2 ounces (60 g) capers
¾ pound (340 g) of
   tomatillos
3 tablespoons butter or oil
   (45 g butter – 42 ml oil)
3 cups (675 ml) chicken
   stock
2 tablespoons (40 g)
   breadcrumbs

Boil chicken in enough salted water to cover for about 45 minutes or until it can be easily disjointed. Reserve the broth from the cooked chicken.

Toast the seeds (don't burn them) over a low flame in a dry pan. Grind the seed and the other ingredients together. It is easier to do the tomatillos in a blender and the rest with a molcajete.

Mix them all together and sauté in the oil for about 10 minutes, stirring occasionally. Stir in 3 cups (675 ml) of the chicken stock. Add the chicken and simmer covered for about 15 minutes. If you desire, you can add breadcrumbs gradually until you reach the thickness you want.

Indian Fried Chicken

Mix the onion, bell pepper, coconut, and garlic with all of the spices.

Rub this mixture into the chicken and let sit for an hour or more.

Fry chicken in oil for 10 minutes.

Add a little water, just enough to keep it simmering rather than frying. Cover and let simmer until done. Check to see that it has enough liquid to keep from sticking.

1 onion, minced
½ bell pepper, minced
2 tablespoons (40 g)
   grated coconut
3 cloves garlic, minced
5 mint leaves, chopped
½ teaspoon (1 g) cayenne,
   or according to taste
⅛ teaspoon (1 g) cinnamon
2 cloves, ground
2 teaspoons (10.6 g)
   ground coriander seeds
½ teaspoon (1 g) turmeric
2½ pounds (1¼ kg)
   chicken, cut in pieces
4 tablespoons (56 ml) oil
Salt

Pollo en Escabeche

Chicken in Onion and Vinegar

5 cloves garlic, crushed
¼ teaspoon (1.5 g) crushed
   cloves (about 6)
1 teaspoon (.5 g) oregano
1 teaspoon (3.3 g) black
   pepper
A good pinch of cinnamon
Salt
5 cups (1125 ml) water
1 large chicken
¼ teaspoon (1 g) allspice
¼ teaspoon (1 g) cumin
5 or 6 peppercorns
5 cloves garlic, peeled and
   roasted
4 mild chiles
5 onions, sliced
¼ cup (56 ml) vinegar

Mix the crushed garlic with half the clove, half the oregano, the black pepper, and cinnamon in water. Add chicken and simmer covered for about 30 minutes.

Remove the chicken and bake at 325° (165°C) for about 30 minutes (until done). It can also be broiled or grilled.

Add the remaining ingredients to the broth used to cook the chicken and let simmer until the onions are done. Leave uncovered so it will cook down until it is not quite soupy. Serve the chicken pieces topped with the onion mixture.

The chicken is often boned before serving. This may require boiling the chicken along with the onion broth.

Pollo Pibil

Chicken Baked in Banana Leaves

Pibil is Mayan for "pit." Cooking chicken in a pit is an ancient culinary custom with the Maya people, but an oven is a lot handier for most people who find the old way too much work.

Sauté the onion in about 1 tablespoon (14 ml) butter or oil until tender.

Cut the chicken in half lengthwise and baste with the remaining oil. Lay a chicken half on a banana leaf and smear it with half the achiote paste. Salt and distribute the onions on both sides. Roll the banana leaf around it, sealing it as best you can. Lay this on a piece of aluminum foil and roll and crimp until it's completely sealed. Bake in a 350° (180°C) oven for about an hour. Longer will not hurt. It can be done on a cookie sheet or on the grate in the oven.

When done, the juice should be drained (it's well worth saving for rice or whatever) and the chicken served on the banana leaf on a plate. A half chicken makes an average serving. The banana leaf can be omitted with a loss of esotericism and a subtle loss of flavor.

1 onion, sliced thin
3 tablespoons butter or oil (45 g butter - 42 ml oil)
1 chicken (a small chicken is best for allowing the spices to permeate)
2 banana leaves
Achiote paste to taste
1 teaspoon (1 g) *azafrán* or Mexican saffron mixed with the achiote paste (optional)

Pollo Asado con Sopa de Fideos

Chicken with Vermicelli

1 chicken
2 cloves garlic, crushed or
  minced
2 sprigs cilantro, pinched
  into pieces
Pinch of oregano
1 onion, coarsely chopped
½ teaspoon (1.5 g) pepper
Salt
Achiote paste
¾ pound (340 g) vermicelli

The chicken can be quartered when raw but will be easier after simmering.

Put everything but the achiote paste and vermicelli in a pot. Cover and simmer about hour (less if already quartered). Remove the chicken and coat the pieces with achiote paste. Salt and cook in a 350° (180°C) oven, broiler, or over a grill until done, about ½ hour, being careful not to let them dry out.

Cook the vermicelli in the water used to cook the chicken. Serve the chicken with vermicelli on the side.

Pollo en Adobo Blanco al Naranja

Chicken in Spices with Orange Juice

The recado for this dish is called recado en adobo blanco. Recado is a Yucatán term for a certain mixture of spices dissolved in vinegar or sour orange.

Boil chicken in salted water for about hour. Remove from water.

Put all of the *recado* ingredients except the vinegar in a hot, dry frying pan or on a *comal*. Toast for about 5 minutes; do not burn to ashes. Grind in a *molcajete* until it becomes paste-like. Add vinegar and mix in a *molcajete* until it's a spreadable paste. (*Recados* can be wrapped and saved for a long time.)

Roast the onions and head of garlic as in iguana sauce.

Spread the *recado* over the chicken and put in a pot. Add the orange juice and the rest of the ingredients. It might be a good idea to add ½ cup (113 ml) or more of the chicken stock to keep it from drying out.

Simmer covered until done, about ½ hour.

Serve with rice and sliced avocado.

Recado en Adobo Blanco

1 chicken
6 small onions (or the equivalent)
1 small head garlic
Juice of 4 oranges
¼ pound (115 g) ham, sliced
1 bell pepper, seeded and sliced
2 *xcatic* chiles, whole (A Hungarian woman who lives in the Yucatán says she thinks that a *xcatic* is the same as a Hungarian banana pepper.)
4 tablespoons (14 g) raisins
2 tablespoons (30 g) capers
¼ teaspoon (1 g) nutmeg
1 tablespoon (15 g) butter
Salt

RECADO
4 cloves garlic
2 onions
6 leaves oregano
5 cloves
3 sticks cinnamon
¼ teaspoon (.5 g) cumin
¼ teaspoon (1.5 g) cilantro seeds
Vinegar, about 1 teaspoon (5 ml)

Mole Colita de San Cristobal

Chicken in Chile Ancho

1 chicken
About 8 inches (20 cm) of
   French bread, cut into
   ½ inch (1½ cm) slices, *no
   problema* if dry
About ½ cup (112 ml) oil
7 *ancho* or *pasilla* chiles,
   the deep red ones,
   deveined and seeded
4 *guajillo* chiles, deveined
   and seeded
Salt
Lettuce and avocado slices
   for garnish

Boil chicken in salted water about 35 minutes. Cut chicken in half.

Fry bread slices in hot oil until they are golden on each side (maybe a minute on each side.) Be careful not to burn. Combine bread with chiles. Grind with a *molcajete* or blend.

Put chiles in boiling water. Turn heat off and allow to soak 25 minutes or so. Blend or grind with a *molcajete*. Strain through a colander with a little water used to cook the chiles. Mash through everything but the peels. Mix the breadcrumbs with the chile if you used a *molcajete*.

You should have enough paste to coat both chicken halves. Add a little chile water or stock, if necessary, to make enough. Salt.

Bake in a 350° (180°C) oven about 25 minutes.

Crepas de Pollo con Chile Chipotle y Nuez

Chicken Crêpes With Chipotle Chiles and Walnuts

Crêpes can be bought frozen in some supermarkets in the United States. They can also be made with pancake mix or by following the other recipe below.

For Pancake Mix Crêpe

Combine ingredients and beat until smooth. The batter will be thinner than for a pancake, and the end product should be thinner.

It's not much more trouble to make "start from scratch" crêpes.

Combine in blender and blend 1 minute. Scrape down the sides and blend 15 seconds more. Refrigerate batter at least an hour. Cook as a pancake, about 20–30 seconds on each side, until the sides start pulling away.

The ingredients will probably make about 10 crêpes. Put a cloth over them to keep them warm until ready to use.

Fill crêpes with shredded chicken and sour cream. Roll up.

Place side by side in a lightly greased baking dish.

Blend walnuts, cream, chiles, and salt in a blender, adding just enough chicken stock to make it liquid enough to pour over crêpes; 1 cup (225 ml) chicken stock should be more than enough.

Bake about 25 minutes in a 300° (150°C) oven until hot and bubbly.

½ chicken, boiled, boned, and shredded
½ cup (112 ml) sour cream
1 cup (92 g) shelled walnuts
1 cup (225 ml) cream
2 chiles *chipotle en adobo* without seeds (This was what Marcela said to use. I used about 6 chiles, ¾ to 1 inch long (2 cm–2½ cm). I also used about ½ teaspoon (1.2 g) of the thick sauce from the can of *chipotle* chiles.)
Salt
Chicken stock (if needed)

PANCAKE MIX CRÊPE BATTER

3 tablespoons (4 ml) oil
3 eggs
1½ cups (337 ml) milk
1½ cups (350 g) pancake mix

CRÊPE BATTER

¼ cup (56 ml) melted butter or oil
3 eggs
2 cups (280 g) flour
2 cups (450 ml) milk
¼ teaspoon (1.5 g) salt

Chiles Rellenos de Pollo or Puerco

Chiles Stuffed with Chicken or Pork

1 pound (450 g) chicken or loin of pork
2 tablespoons (28 ml) oil
3 tomatoes, chopped
1 onion, chopped
3 cloves garlic, minced
12 olives, chopped
¼ teaspoon (.25 g) oregano
2 tablespoons (12.5 g) parsley, finely chopped
10-12 chiles *Oaxaqueños* or chiles *de agua* (These are names for the same chile. It does not exist outside of Oaxaca. Outside of Oaxaca, chile *poblanos* are usually used for stuffing.)
4 eggs
About 1 cup (140 g) flour
About ½ cup (70 g) breadcrumbs
About ½ cup (112 ml) liquid used to cook the meat
Salt

Boil chicken or pork in salted water 40 minutes to 1 hour, a little longer for pork. Remove from water, let cool, and shred.

Fry the tomato, onion, garlic, olives, oregano, and parsley in oil for about 10 minutes.

Heat the chiles in a dry pan until they darken, but do not burn. Roll them in a damp cloth and leave until they cool. Slit down the sides and remove the seeds and veins. Stuff with the meat.

Separate the eggs. Beat the whites until stiff. Beat the yolks. Mix together and stir slightly.

Dip chiles in flour, egg, breadcrumbs.

Put in hot oil at least ¼ inch (1 cm) deep and fry, turning until light brown all over. Put chiles on paper towels to absorb the oil. Stir as much stock as necessary into the tomato mixture for sauce to cover the chiles. Pour over the chiles and serve.

Tamales de Pollo o Puerco

Chicken or Pork Tamales

This should make around 15 tamales.

Devein and seed chiles. Put in water and boil for 5 minutes. Grind in a *molcajete*.

Boil chicken or pork in salted water for 40 minutes. When cool, pull into small pieces (not finely shredded).

Put flour and cooled stock, enough to make a thick liquid, in a pot. Stir until smooth. Add butter and heat, stirring until it gets thick. Sometimes some of the ground chile is mixed into the *masa*. If this is done, you might use an extra chile. The number of chiles used is largely a matter of personal discretion anyway.

Lay banana leaf on a flat surface. If using avocado leaves, lay one in the center. They give a slight anise flavor to the tamale. Put about 2 tablespoons (30 g) *masa* in the center and let flow over the leaf. You might have to help it to spread. Leave about 1 inch (2 cm) on the sides and a little more on the ends.

You can dunk the meat in the stock to moisten it. Put a little meat in the center of the banana leaf and elongate it to roughly dictate the length of the tamale. Put a little tomato, onion, chile, and *epazote* leaves over the meat. Sprinkle with salt.

Fold one side over the meat (do not roll), then the other. Fold the ends the opposite way to make a seal.

Tie with string, lengthwise and across.

Put in steamer and cook 45 minutes to 1 hour. When the tamales are done the *masa* will not stick to the leaves.

3 *ancho* chiles
1 pound (450 g) boneless pork, or 1 chicken
Salt
1½ pounds (680 g) masa flour
3 sticks butter, margarine, or lard
Banana leaves cut into 12 inch x 8 inch (30 cm x 21½ cm) pieces, without the center rib (fresh are better than dried, as they offer some flavor)
Avocado leaves (optional)
½ pound (225 g) tomatoes, cut in half and sliced thin
1 small onion, cut in half and sliced thin
Several sprigs *epazote*
String, or strings from the ribs of the banana leaves

Pavo en Relleno Blanco

Turkey Stuffed with Ground Pork in White Sauce

**1 turkey, about 10 pounds
(4 ½ kg)**
Epazote
Cloves

FOR THE STUFFING
8 cloves garlic, minced
½ teaspoon (1 g) allspice
½ teaspoon (1 g) cumin
**3 tablespoons (30 g) black
pepper**
¼ teaspoon (1 g) cinnamon
1 teaspoon (.6 g) oregano
Salt
2 pounds (1 kg) ground pork
5 tomatoes, chopped
1 large onion, chopped
**1 tablespoon (15 g) capers,
rinsed if salty**
15 olives, chopped
2 tablespoons (30 g) raisins
**2 tablespoons (12 g)
ground almonds**
2 raw eggs
**4 hard boiled eggs, whites
finely chopped**

FOR THE TOMATO SAUCE
3 tablespoons (42 ml) oil
2 onions, chopped
8 tomatoes, chopped
2 chiles *xcatic*
2 tablespoons raisins
10 olives, chopped
1 tablespoon (8.75 g)capers

Boil the turkey as in recipe for *gallipava,* but with the addition of a sprig of *epazote* and 4 cloves.

Mix the garlic and spices. Keep aside half.

Sauté the meat with half the spices, tomatoes, and onion until meat is done and vegetables are soft. Add the capers, olives, raisins, and almonds. Let cool.

Beat the 2 raw eggs, and mix into the meat, along with the chopped egg whites.

Distribute the yolks throughout the stuffing and stuff the turkey. Sew the cavity closed.

Put salt and the remainder of the garlic and spices on turkey, and roast as in recipe for *gallipava.*

For the tomato sauce:

Fry all the ingredients in oil for about 10 minutes, or until it becomes a sauce.

Make a *kol* as in the recipe for *queso relleno,* using the stock from the turkey. You might prefer the *kol* to be a little thinner.

To serve, put some meat from the turkey in a bowl with some of the stuffing. Pour *kol* over it and then tomato sauce.

Pavo en Relleno Negro

Stuffed Turkey in Blackened Chile Sauce

Peculiar as it seems, the chiles are burned until they are black all the way through and turn to ashes. The whole chile can be used, even the stem. Hot New Mexico chiles are good because burning takes away most of the heat and leaves a rich flavor. The burning should be done outside—the flaming chiles give off a lot of strong smoke. Roast over a grill until completely blackened. Sometimes 6 to a dozen tortillas are burned and their ashes added to those of the chiles, but this is optional and more often not done.

Grind or smash the chile ashes in a bag to make a powder. Mix with the pepper, salt, allspice, cumin, annatto seeds, oregano, and crushed garlic in 4 cups (900 ml) of water. Strain this mixture in a colander, adding water if necessary. Do not be discouraged if it is black and gritty and ridiculous-looking; it is supposed to be like that, and the cooking smooths it out.

Slice 5 of the tomatoes and sauté them with the onion and *epazote* leaves in butter. Add the pork and simmer along with 1 cup (225 ml) of the strained chile mixture. When the meat is done, let it cool.

Beat the raw eggs. Chop fine the cooked egg whites. Add salt and mix with the pork. Distribute the hard-boiled egg yolks here and there in the mixture and stuff the turkey. Close the cavity by sewing or with skewers.

Salt the turkey and put it in a large pot to boil. Pour the rest of the strained chile mixture over the turkey. If necessary, add enough water to immerse ¾ of the turkey. Cover and simmer until about half done, 1½ to 2 hours. Add the rest of the tomatoes, cut in half, add the epazote branches. Cover and continue to simmer, removing the cover the last hour or so to allow the black liquid to cook down and thicken.

This dish is likely to require more practice than most, but if it comes out right it is very unusual and very savory. The meat should be permeated with a mild heat from the chiles. A chicken can be used instead of a turkey, adjusting proportions and time accordingly.

2 pounds (1 kg) large dried chiles
2 tablespoons (20 g) black pepper
Salt
¼ teaspoon (1 g) allspice
¼ teaspoon (.5 g) cumin (3 or 4 good pinches)
2 tablespoons (30 g) crushed *annatto* seeds
6 good pinches oregano
12 cloves garlic, crushed
12 tomatoes
1 onion, chopped
1 tablespoon (15 g) crushed *epazote* leaves, and about 6 inches (15 cm) (total) *epazote* stems
2 tablespoons (30 g) butter
2 raw eggs
4 hard boiled eggs
2 pounds (1 kg) ground pork
1 medium turkey, 10-15 pounds (4½–6½ kg)

Gallipava

Chicken Estrella Family Style

When I arrived at the Rosado's, Doña María and Emanuela were at a sink in the backyard scrubbing the *gallipava* with limes. It had gotten a little old, and they were rejuvenating it.

Emanuela put the *gallipava* in a large pot with enough water to cover it, and turned on the fire. When it started boiling, Doña María added about 5 cloves of roasted garlic, 1 teaspoon (2.39 g) pepper, about 1 tablespoon (20 g) dried oregano leaves, and salt.

While the chicken was boiling it was *botana* and beer time. Baked tortilla chips were put on the table. The dinner table was used for kitchen work, and Doña María now used it to make a dip for the chips—*hasikilpac.* It was well worth making.

The *gallipava* boiled 1¼ hours. It was put on a platter on the dining table. I had brought a bag of achiote paste that I had bought at the central market. There is a *recado* monger there. They make all of the Yucatán *recados* themselves. I asked Doña María if it was better than La Anita, the most common store-bought brand.

"*Sí,*" she said, "*Es mas alegre, viva mas.*" (It is more cheerful, more alive.)

She mixed about 3 tablespoons (45 g) of the paste with enough vinegar to make it thick, then basted the *gallipava* inside and out. Manuela put it on the charcoal that Doña María had lit. She turned it about every 15 minutes. After 1¼ hours, it was pronounced done. It was a deep red brown all over, very pretty so far as a bird ready to be eaten goes.

Tortillas, black beans mashed to a paste, lettuce, a bowl of sliced onion and tomatoes, and a bowl of sliced white onion in vinegar accompanied the *gallipava. Longaniza de Valladolid* that had been cooked over the charcoal was also served. Soup was made with macaroni and broth remaining from boiling the *gallipava.*

EAST OF MÉRIDA, WEST OF CANCUN

The meaning of the word *vicho* varies from one Spanish-speaking country to another. In some places, a lover is called *vicho*. In others, people use the word when referring to an animal, as if to say, "Aw, poor thing." In southern Mexico, a cat is sometimes called *el vicho*. The word is also used to describe an object one might step on, such as an unappealing bug. How Don Vicente of Dzilam de Bravo acquired his *apodo* (nickname) of Vicho is anybody's guess.

I met Vicho by circumstance one Sunday night on one of my early trips to Mexico when the coconut palms were still beautiful. While in Dzilam de Bravo, the easternmost *puerto* on Yucatán's coastal highway, a friend and I had decided to get a six-pack of beer, sit on the picturesque sea wall bordering the Gulf of Mexico near Mérida, and listen to music. The beer, however, was not easy to come by. In the Yucatán, restaurants are the only establishments permitted to sell alcohol on Sundays, and in Dzilam de Bravo these were nowhere to be found. Finally, someone told us to try the hotel—to knock if the door wasn't open. Indeed, there was no sign of life at the Hotel Flamingo, so I knocked on a shutter. A man appearing to be in his sixties opened the window and stuck his head out. It was Vicho.

"*Se vende cerveza?*" I asked.

"*Si,*" he answered, motioning us to come around to the restaurant at the back of the building.

After letting us in through the kitchen door, he opened two bottled beers and set them on a table. Looking in the refrigerator, he asked if we wanted some lobster or octopus. Although we said no, he took out a piece of octopus and began chopping. Next he chopped tomato, onion, cilantro, and *habanero* chile, tossing all the ingredients together. He squeezed lime over the mixture, sprinkled it with salt, thrust two forks in it, and placed it in front of us.

My request for beer had turned into a party in the kitchen of the Hotel Flamingo's restaurant—a little fiesta complete with beer, *pulpo a la mexicano* (octopus seviche) (p. 15), and conversation. Tourist attractions are hard to find in Dzilam de Bravo, said Vicho, but one could take a boat ride to see flamingos or catch fish in shallow water, using nets just like the ancient Maya did. As for Vicho, he had, in addition to the only hotel in town, a boat, a video camera, a large number of acquaintances, and what turned out to be a gnawing loneliness.

He offered us a room at the hotel "for free." He wanted us to stay so badly that it was hard to leave him, but we did. I told him I would come again soon.

The following Sunday I returned to the Hotel Flamingo. Vicho was glad to see me and later joined me at a table in his *palapa* restaurant. The only other guests at the hotel were also sitting under the *palapa,* sipping brandy, and using a camping stove to cook fish they had caught earlier in the day.

After watching them for a moment, Vicho turned to me and explained that he was glad I had come in late summer because it was octopus season. During this time of year, he said, one can rarely find crab to eat because it is used as bait for the octopus. But before octopus season, crabmeat is sold by the kilo at a very reasonable price. Then he invited me into the kitchen once again.

This time I was able to sit and talk with the seventy-five year old cook, Otilio, as he prepared *botanas* for the Sunday afternoon crowd that was beginning to filter in. He was making *pulpo en su tinta* (octopus in its ink) (p. 15) and *pulpo en escabeche* (octopus in vinegar) (p. 16). As he peeled and diced the octopus, I told him that the fried fish along the Yucatán coast was the best I had ever eaten. He said the fish are tasty because they are so fresh, and they are especially good in Dzilam de Bravo because, with its off-shore reef, the fish are able to feed on small fish and plant life from the reef.

As soon as the *botanas* were ready, Otilio told me how to make *pescado frito entero* (whole fried fish) (p. 182). It was a whole-fish recipe very common along the coast.

Then Vicho appeared in the kitchen to say he wanted to show me some beach property just outside of Dzilam de Bravo. It was to be a minor resort, and a portion of the property—a large lot close to the beach—was available for $4,000. The lot, it turned out, was about 100 yards by 100 feet and teeming with coconut palms. It was very pretty and very tempting.

Totolandia

Although I was not aware of it at the time, the Hotel Flamingo and its owner were to become part of my Yucatán tour. Whenever a friend flew in to Cancún's airport from the United States, I would insist on a quick getaway from Cancún and a stopover at the Hotel Flamingo on our way to Mérida. Vicho always greeted my friends enthusiastically and would occasionally invite us to the local disco or to a *baile* (dance) in his hometown of Dzidzantún. Sometimes after delivering my homebound guests to the airport in Cancún, I would also return to Mérida by way of Vicho's hotel.

On one such return journey from Cancún, I spent the night at the Hotel Flamingo and, early in the morning, drove off to find some coffee. What I found was Totolandia, the new resort on the beachside property Vicho had shown me years before.

Totolandia was quite rustic. Six cabins had been built helter-skelter around a restaurant. In the dining area of the restaurant were tables and chairs set on the sand under a *palapa* (roof); the kitchen, with its concrete floor, was under a tin roof.

All the beautiful coconut trees were turning brown and dying—victims of *amarillamiento letal* (lethal yellow), a disease that attacks the centers of trees. The epidemic was said to have hit Jamaica in the 1930s and Florida in the 1960s. Having whirled in with Hurricane Gilberto in 1988, it was now devastating thousands of coconut palms along the Yucatán coast.

A man and woman sitting at a table introduced themselves as Toto and Flor and invited me to join them. Toto, a man of German and Mexican descent, had a ruddy complexion, white hair, and more weight than his large frame could comfortably hold. His Mexican wife Flor, also heavyset, had a pretty face. At the table were their three daughters, who ranged in age from twelve to twenty-one.

We talked about the hurricane. Boats had been found more than half a mile inland from Dzilam de Bravo. Portions of the road to Progreso were still missing, and hundreds of beach homes were in disrepair.

Toto went on to say that his father, a botanist, had come from Germany in the 1920s to study the flora of the Yucatán. He settled in Izamal, forty-five miles inland. Toto was proud to say that his father owned the first car in the state of Yucatán. Going into the family living quarters, he reappeared with a photograph of his father standing next to a Model T Ford.

While Toto was off looking for the photo, Flor and I talked about favorite recipes. Then she explained that she and her husband were celebrating their thirtieth anniversary that day—many people would be coming, the food would be delicious, and I was welcome to join them. Most of the other guests, she added, were siblings and their families.

Within minutes, people began arriving and hugging one another, glad to be together for this occasion. In the midst of the crowd was an upper-middle-aged couple from the United States who introduced themselves to me as people who had been living in Izamal for many years. The woman, Diane, was Toto's partner in Totolandia. With her husband she shared another business venture—a retirement home for "well-heeled Americans" in Izamal. She indicated that it was very lucrative.

Diane pointed out Toto's two sisters and his brother Wilo. Another brother, Adolfo, would not be coming, she explained, because he was the family drunk and rarely left his home in Izamal.

"Wilo's wife, Marta, makes the best *queso relleno* (stuffed cheese) (p. 108)," she said. "Try it."

I did, and it was superb.

Soon after I returned to my seat, Wilo sat beside me. He was tall and thin and had acquired his father's interest in the flora of the region. He explained that virtually all the coconut palms were going to die. Although they could be saved by penicillin, he said, such an effort would be too expensive for the government to undertake. Instead, the entire coast would have to be reforested. Scientists, he added, had cultivated a coconut tree that was resistant to lethal yellow. This new breed of tree was a cross between a Panamanian giant and a Malaysian dwarf.

Wilo was fascinated by plant life, but his real passion, it turned out, was for Datsuns. He owned a Datsun repair shop in Izamal and spent much of his time fixing and remodeling cars. When I told him my brother had been a factory-team Datsun driver, we forged an immediate camaraderie. After a good conversation about Datsuns, he invited me to visit him in Izamal. *Mi casa, tu casa.*

That was when the *botanas* were served. First came *pan de cazón* (p. 17). Believed to have originated in Campeche, this minced shark "tortilla sandwich" is prepared throughout the Yucatán Peninsula. Accompanying the shark were sliced beets and red onion marinated in lime, chopped boiled potatoes with peas, and sliced boiled carrots marinated in vinegar.

When it came time to leave for Mérida, I thanked Toto and Flor and wished them many more happy anniversaries. Flor, in turn, handed me her recipe for octopus soup. Substituting one ink fish for another, I have on many occasions prepared *sopa de calamar* (squid soup (p. 53).

Izamal

Izamal is nothing like Mérida. The latter was once called "The White City," but the name no longer applies. The former, "The Yellow City," is still yellow. Izamal's large yellow convent was built in the mid-sixteenth century less than a mile from one of the largest ancient Maya structures—the Pyramid of Kinich Kakmo. Izamal is also a tranquil city that permits horses to pull their carriages in peace.

Finding Wilo in Izamal was easy: I simply asked for the Datsun mechanic. He remembered me from Toto and Flor's anniversary fiesta and was glad I had taken him up on his offer to visit. He showed me around his repair shop with gusto, then whisked me off to his house for turkey tacos. The turkey was left over from *pavo en relleno blanco* (stuffed turkey in white sauce) (p. 160), which he had had the day before for dinner. Although the dish is traditionally made with turkey, his wife had used chicken.

While we were at his house, Wilo insisted on showing me a picture of his father with his Model T Ford. It was the same photograph Toto had shown me. They were certainly proud of their father's car. Wilo's next desire was to show me around Izamal and introduce me to some of his other relatives. But first we needed to go back to the shop so he could tell his assistant he would be out for a while. With that task accomplished, we set off in his Datsun for an interesting and different tour of Izamal.

It was both fun and educational. Perhaps not realizing that I was having a hard enough time speaking and understanding Spanish, Wilo began to teach me words in Maya. In the course of visiting Wilo's many relatives, I frequented a variety of backyard gardens. I saw an *annatto* tree, producer of the *achiote* seed. I saw a papaya tree, as well as a sour orange, sour lime, and banana tree. I saw *epazote* growing, and also *orégano, hierbabuena* (mint), *cebollinas,* chiles *habaneros,* chiles *xcatic, calabazas,* and *mélons.* Wilo showed me all these crops with great exuberance.

Finally he told me, with excitement in his voice, that we were going to visit his brother Adolfo. Wilo had a sense of enthusiasm that seemed to include everyone and everything. He was very aware of his surroundings.

"Adolfo likes rum," he said, then added, "I used to drink brandy, rum, and tequila, but now I only drink beer. Adolfo has never been married, but then he has had a lot of girlfriends."

Adolfo's house was not as nice as the others we had seen that day. When we arrived, he was sitting at a table in his back room, drinking rum and Coke. The room was stark. A naked lightbulb hung on a wire from the ceiling, illuminating the concrete floor and concrete-block walls. The only furniture visible was the table and four chairs. Many empty rum bottles were in a corner of the room; more were on the table. Adolfo was pleased that his brother had come to visit.

Adolfo had a craggy face, appearing as if the skin of an eighty-five year old had been draped over sixty-year-old bones. Many families have their social dropouts, and he was clearly one.

The conversation soon turned to food, my main interest in meeting Adolfo. I asked him if he knew how to make *lomitos de Valladolid* (pork stew from Valladolid) (p. 109), a dish I had heard about. He did and told me all the ingredients. Then, proud of his home state, he went on to give me a recipe for *pezuñas con garbanzos* (pig's feet) (p. 122).

PESCADOS

The fish and seafood of the Yucatán coast are some of the best in the world. Many nutrient rich rivers and streams flow into the shallow waters of the coast. The long coral reef is teeming with marina life. Combined with these blessings, the water is still fresh and clear.

Pescado con Chile Ancho y Jugo de Naranja

Fish with Ancho Chile and Orange Juice

2 *ancho* chiles
1½ pounds (¾ kg) fish
　fillets, sliced
Salt and pepper
½ teaspoon (.3 g) oregano
Oil
5 tomatoes
1 small onion
2 cloves garlic
1 orange

Bring chiles to a boil and let cool in the water.

Sprinkle fish with salt, pepper, and oregano, and fry in hot oil until brown.

Blend the tomatoes, onion, garlic, and chiles. Fry in the same oil used to cook the fish for 10 minutes.

Add the fish and juice from the orange, and allow to come to a boil.

Remove from heat and serve with sliced radishes, sliced *jalapeño* chiles, and shredded lettuce on the side.

Caserola de Pescado con Nopales

Fish Casserole with Nopal

If canned nopals are used, they should be rinsed before using. Fresh nopals are better. They can be bought in some markets. Remove the spines. Boil in salted water about 30-40 minutes until they do not squeak when chewed. Cut into strips ⅓ by ¾ inch (1-2 cm).

Layer the fish on the bottom of a greased baking dish and salt it. Put the onion slices over the fish, then the nopals, garlic, and butter. Repeat, creating more layers depending on the amount of ingredients. Bake at 275°(135°C) for 20 to 30 minutes or until the fish is done. It can be served with rice and slices of avocado.

2 pounds (1 kg) fish fillet
3 cups (420 g) nopals
1 medium onion sliced thin
2 cloves garlic, minced
2 tablespoons (30 g) butter
Salt to taste

Pen Chuc

Salted Fish Cooked on Coals

Put fish directly on charcoal. Cook about 10 minutes on each side.

Another way to cook a whole fish is *a la sal*. Put about ¼ inch (½ cm) salt in a *comal* or frying pan, put the fish on top of this, and cover with salt. Cook a few minutes until done.

1 fish, cleaned, but not scaled
Salt

Tikinxik Cubano

Whole Fish Grilled with Chile and Beer

1 large tomato, chopped
Onion
½ bell pepper, chopped
2 chiles *xcatic*, chopped
Oil
2 ounces (56 g)
  recado colorado
Lime
Salt
1 6- to 7-pound (3-3½ kg)
  fish for 5 people,
  opened by cutting
  through back
¼ bottle of beer, preferably
  dark

Although he was not a cook by profession, Otilo said that people who come to the restaurant often say, "We want Cubano to cook." I asked how he makes tikinxik. On a piece of paper from my notebook, he drew a fish that had been sliced open through the back. He folded the paper double, making the fish whole, then opened it, indicating that the fish had been cut open. Then he drew slits running lengthwise on the inside of the fish. The slits are so the fish will absorb the sauce.

Fry the tomato, onion, bell pepper, and chiles until they are soft and become a sauce.

Dissolve the *recado* with lime and salt. He said it is very important that the *recado* is only achiote, lime, and salt, not like what can be bought in markets. Mix with the tomato sauce.

Cook fish 8 inches (20 cm) from charcoal on the opened side 15 to 20 minutes.

Turn and spread the sauce over the inside of the fish. Shake a bottle of beer and squirt about ¼ of it over the sauce. Cook on the opened side 10 minutes.

Cubano kissed the ends of his fingers, indicating that his *tikinxic* is exquisite. He mentioned a manner in which he cooks shrimp. He blends shrimp and lobster shells with lime juice until it is a sauce. He puts this on the shrimp and sautés them until they are done. (Be sure to remove the shells before eating.)

Macum Verde

Fish Casserole with Fresh Oregano

Put a layer of fish slices in a greased casserole dish. Grind the oregano and other spices with a *molcajete* until fine, and put over fish.

Put the onion slices over this. Add ⅓ cup (75 ml) water or stock, only enough to cover the bottom of the dish.

Add salt and bake in a 300° (150°C) oven for 20 minutes.

2 pounds (1 kg) fish, cut crosswise in slices
2 tablespoons (28 g) lard or butter
1 to 1½ cups (227-340 g) fresh oregano leaves
3 balls allspice
8 peppercorns
2 small heads garlic
⅛ teaspoon (.5 g) cumin
2 cloves
1 medium onion, sliced
Salt

Filete Macumba

Breaded and Fried Fish Fillet

2½ pounds (1¼ kg) fish
  fillet
1 sour orange
Salt
Pepper
3 eggs, beaten
Flour
Oil
½ bell pepper, cut in thin
  strips
2 balls allspice, coarsely
  ground
5 bay leaves
1 chile *xcatic*, cut in rings
1 medium red onion,
  sliced thin and cut in
  half
5 tomatoes, sliced and cut
  in half
1 teaspoon (5 ml) bottled
  chile sauce
1 tablespoon (14 g) butter
1 tablespoon (14 g)
  mayonnaise
Radishes

Otilo said that many people order this during la temporada.

Marinate the fillets 2 or 3 minutes with juice from the orange, salt, and pepper. Dip the fillets in the egg and then flour two times. Fry in oil, turning until golden on both sides.

Fry the bell pepper, chile, onion, tomato, and bottled chile sauce in a little oil until everything is soft. Stir in the butter and mayonnaise. Put over the fish and serve with radishes on the side.

Makum de Pescado

Fish Casserole with Achiote

Dissolve the achiote in the juice of the sour orange and vinegar. Cut the fish into strips and cover with achiote paste.

Sauté the bell pepper, onion, and garlic until it begins to get soft, about 5 minutes.

Salt fish and put in a greased baking dish (can also be cooked if covered on top of the stove). Put the vegetables on top, and bake in a 325°(165°C) oven for 25 minutes until done.

7 ounces (200 g) of packaged achiote (or its equivalent, if you make your own)
2 sour oranges
½ cup (118 ml) vinegar
1½ pounds (¾ kg) fish fillets
Oil
2 bell peppers, cut into thin round slices
1 onion, thinly sliced
3 cloves garlic, minced
Salt
3 tomatoes, sliced
3 tablespoons (28 g) chopped parsley

Pescado a la Talla

Grilled Fish with Achiote

1 fish with head, scaled
    and cleaned
Achiote, to taste
Sour orange
Lime
Salt

Large fish 16 inches (41 cm) and more are cooked this way.

Baste fish inside and out with achiote paste mixed with sour orange juice and lime. Salt.

Cook over an open grill for about 20 minutes, or until done, turning constantly. It is necessary to be delicate when turning the fish so that it doesn't break. The outside should turn brown and have a little bit of a crust when it is considered done.

Pescado en Adobo

Fish Sautéed in Chile Sauce

Prepare chiles as in recipe for oyster soup. Roast the tomatoes. Mix the tomatoes, garlic, onion, and spices in a *molcajete* or blender and fry for 10 minutes.

Add fish and simmer 15 minutes until done.

Served surrounded by lettuce and sliced radishes.

4 *ancho* **chiles**
4 Italian tomatoes
1 small onion
2 cloves garlic
½ teaspoon (2 g) oregano
⅛ teaspoon (.5 g) cinnamon
2 tablespoons (30 g) oil
1½ pounds (3/4 kg) fish fillets
Lettuce
Radishes
Salt

Pescado Relleno con Salsa de Queso

Fish Stuffed with Cheese Sauce

1, 2- to 3-pound (1-1½ kg) fish with head (some people in the U.S. prefer to have the head cut off)
Juice of 1 to 1½ limes
Salt
½ pound (227 g) of Oaxacan cheese (or Monterrey Jack)
1 tablespoon (28 g) butter
1 medium tomato, chopped
1 medium onion, chopped
2 cloves garlic, minced
1 branch of cilantro, chopped

Marinate the fish ½ hour in the lime and salt. Shred cheese. Melt the butter and mix all the ingredients together. Salt and stir. Stuff the fish with the mixture, and close with toothpicks. Bake at 250° (120°C) for 25 minutes to ½ hour.

Pescado al Horno en Rojo

Fish Baked with Achiote and Wine

Fish is sold in hundreds of places along the paved road of the Yucatán coast. It can be found in restaurants, homes with hand-painted signs, and places in between. It is the best fish I have ever had.

Baste the fish with the *recado colorado*. Salt.

Put a banana leaf on a baking pan. Put the *tikinxik* (the open basted fish) on the banana leaf or tin foil.

Put the sliced vegetables on top, and cover with another banana leaf. Pour the wine around the fish and bake in a 350° (180°C) oven for 20 to 30 minutes or until done.

1, 18 inch (46 cm) fish, opened from the back
Recado colorado to cover fish
Salt
2 banana leaves
2 tomatoes, thinly sliced lengthwise
1 large onion, thinly sliced lengthwise
1 small bell pepper, thinly sliced lengthwise
¾ pound (340 g) potatoes, boiled and sliced
⅓ bottle white wine

Caserola de Pescado y Camarones con Crema

Fish and Shrimp Casserole

2 pounds (1 kg) fish fillets
Margarine to fry fish
½ pound (¼ kg) shrimp
Large can mushrooms,
   drained
1 large onion, chopped
1 bell pepper, seeded,
   deveined, and chopped
1 pound (½ kg) tomatoes,
   chopped
½ pound (¼ kg) cheese
   that melts
¾ stick margarine or
   butter
½ cup (113 g) flour
1 cup (237 ml) milk
6 ounces (170 g) heavy
   cream
3 eggs
Salt
Pepper

Fry fish in margarine until white, about 5 minutes. Make room for shrimp on one side of frying pan, and add them the last 2 minutes. Add mushrooms without the juice.

Cover the bottom of a greased casserole dish with fish. Add a layer of shrimp. Put the rest of the fish and shrimp aside, keeping them more or less separated.

Fry ½ of onion, bell pepper, and tomatoes for 5 minutes in the oil used to fry the fish. Add more butter or margarine if necessary.

Put a layer of sauce over shrimp.

Put a layer of cheese over sauce. Repeat layers until ingredients are gone, ending with a layer of sauce on top.

Fry remaining onion and cup flour with ¾ stick margarine. Continue stirring until flour is just a little brown. Add milk. Turn heat down and stir. Add cream.

Separate eggs and beat whites until fluffy. Stir in yolks. Stir eggs into sauce.

Put sauce on top of fish and bake in a 300°(150°C) oven for about 20 minutes.

Sancoche de Pescado

Fish Fillet with Mashed Potatoes

Grind allspice and cloves. Add with salt and bay leaves to water to cover fish. Simmer fish 5 minutes. Let fish cool in water so it can be removed whole.

Boil potatoes and mash. Stir in butter, pepper, canned and powdered milk. Otilio said to squeeze in lime juice until it tastes like cheese.

Remove the backbone from fish.

Fill the fish with the potatoes. Put the rest on top. Add the can of chiles and peas.

3 balls allspice
3 cloves
Salt
5 bay leaves
1 18 inch (46 cm) fish (snapper or snook are best)
2 pounds (1 kg) potatoes
½ pound (225 g) butter
Pepper
1 small can evaporated milk
Lime juice
6 tablespoons (120 g) powdered milk
1 small can chiles
1 small can peas, drained

Pescado Frito Entero

Yucatán Whole Fried Fish

Salt
**1 fish, averaging about 12
   inches (30 cm)**
Oil
Lime to marinate fish

Marinate fish in lime juice for a few minutes. Salt fish and put in oil. The oil should cover half of the fish and be hot enough so that it bubbles. The fish should cook quickly to keep its juice in.

Serve on lettuce, surrounded by sliced tomato, onion, and a chopped *habanero* chile.

Chiles Anchos Rellenos de Pescado

Ancho Chiles Filled with Fish

Slit chiles halfway down the sides and remove veins and seeds. Soak for 15 minutes in water just off the boil. Fry tomatoes, 1 onion, and 2 cloves garlic in 2 tablespoons (28 ml) oil for 5 minutes. Add fish, capers, olives, and bay leaf. Simmer uncovered for 20 to 30 minutes, until it cooks down.

After this mixture cools, stuff chiles. Leave enough space in the chile to push the slit closed. Dip chiles in flour, then egg, and fry in hot oil about ½ inch (1½ cm) deep about 6 minutes on each side.

A tomato sauce like one used with fish can be put on top. The sauce that Alberto made was:

Sauté the remaining onion and garlic in a little oil until tender. Add tomato sauce, wine and chicken bouillon and simmer a few minutes. Add a little chicken stock if desired. Served over chiles.

6 to 8 dried *ancho* chiles
2 tablespoons (28 ml) oil
3 tomatoes, chopped
2 onions, chopped
3 cloves garlic, minced
1 pound (450 g) fish fillets, ground or finely chopped
12 capers
15 olives, chopped
1 bay leaf
4 tablespoons (60 g) flour
2 eggs, beaten
1 15-ounce (425 g) can tomato sauce
2 tablespoons (28 ml) red wine
2 teaspoons (12.4 g) powdered chicken bouillon
Salt

Tortillas de Pescado

Fish Omelet

1 onion, chopped
2 tomatoes, chopped
6 olives, chopped
4 capers, rinsed if they are
   extremely salty
Oil
1 pound (450 g) fish fillets
Salt
1 bay leaf
6 eggs, beaten

Fry onion, tomatoes, olives, and capers in oil for 10 minutes. Boil fish in salted water with bay leaf until it is done and flakes easily. Shred finely. Add fish to tomato mixture and sauté until it is almost dry. Mix everything with eggs, and cook in a little oil until eggs are done.

The same recipe can be used with other seafood, such as oysters, shrimp, octopus, and crab.

Pescado Veracruz

Veracruz-Style Fish

Put salt and juice of lime on fish, and allow to marinate about ½ hour.

Heat oil in a skillet and cook onion and garlic until onion is soft. Do not allow to brown. Add the rest of the ingredients and allow to simmer for about 10 to 15 minutes, until the tomatoes have broken down into a sauce. Put fish in the sauce and allow to simmer covered until fish is done, about 10 minutes. Add water as necessary to keep the sauce liquid.

1½ pounds (¾ kg) fish fillets (red snapper is most common)
3 cloves garlic, minced
1 pound (.5 kg) tomatoes, chopped
1 onion, sliced thin
1 cup (227 g) green olives, sliced
1 tablespoon (5 g) capers
2 tablespoons (28 g) canned strips of chiles in vinegar
2 bay leaves
¼ cup (60 ml) olive oil
1 lime
Salt to taste

Quesadillas de Pescado Veracruzana

Fish Quesadillas Veracruz Style

1 pound (.5 kg) fish fillets
Salt
1½ onions
1 clove, ground
1 bay leaf
1 clove garlic, minced
1 tomato
2 *jalapeños*, finely chopped
1 teaspoon (5 ml) vinegar
1 tablespoon (14 g)
   chopped cilantro
Tortillas
Oil

Boil fish in enough salted water to cover it, along with ½ onion, clove, bay leaf, and garlic for 10 minutes. Remove fish, let cool, and shred.

Fry tomato, onion, *jalapeño,* and vinegar in oil for 8 minutes. Add fish and chopped cilantro.

Put fish mixture over half of tortilla, fold over, and fry on each side until it begins to brown. Served with shredded cabbage tossed with lime and mayonnaise.

Pescado Seco Salado

Salted and Dried Fish

Cut through the back of the fish so that it will open out flat. Remove the intestines and gills. Leave the scales. Cut slits across the meat on the inside of the fish. Pack the slits with salt. Rub the rest of the fish with salt. Expose the inside of the fish to the sun, draped over a stick that is parallel to the ground. It is important that the fish is exposed to the sun. After one day, dip the fish in salted water for just a few seconds. Some people do this in the ocean. It supposedly keeps flies off while the fish is drying in the sun. Dry for another 4 or 5 days. (Local superstition says the fish should be brought in at night, not just for obvious reasons, such as animals, but if the moon is in the wrong phase the fish will be no good. It will be mushy.)

For fillets of large fish, such as shark and marlin, skin them and salt both sides of the meat. If they are thick, slit and salt as for whole fish. Expose both sides equally in the sun. When they are dried, they last four or five months.

Pescado Seco Entero

Dried Salted Whole Fish

1, 12 inch (30 cm) fish,
  salted and dried in the
  sun
2 tomatoes
1 *jalapeño* chile
1 clove garlic
1 sprig cilantro
10 green olives, chopped
  (optional)
1 potato, boiled and
  cubed (optional)

Soak fish for ½ hour, and discard water. Do this two times. Grill fish over coals or fry for about 15 minutes on each side.

Roast the tomato as for iguana recipe. Devein chile and blend or grind in *molcajete* with tomato, garlic, and cilantro. Serve fish with sauce on the side.

Filete de Pescado Seco Salado

Dried Salted Fish Fillet

Dried fish fillet,
  12 inches x 6 inches
  (30 cm x 15 cm)
4 tomatoes, chopped
1 onion, chopped
1 bell pepper
1 or 2 *jalapeño* chiles
1 tablespoon (15 ml) oil
1 sour orange

Soak fish as above, or soak overnight. Boil ½ hour in fresh water. Shred meat. Fry all ingredients except fish in 1 tablespoon (15 ml) oil over medium flame for 10 minutes.

Put fish in sauce, add juice of 1 sour orange or a dash vinegar, and simmer covered for 25 minutes.

Salsa de Chile Ancho

Salsa for Dried, Salted Fish

Roast the head of garlic as in recipe for iguana. Boil *ancho* chiles and bell pepper for about 10 minutes; turn off heat and soak 20 to 30 minutes. Blend all the ingredients in a *molcajete*. The seeds will not grind in a blender; they will simply bounce around.

Put fish in the sauce and simmer covered for 25 minutes.

1 head of garlic
3 or 4 dried *ancho* chiles, stemmed and deveined
1 chile *dulce* or bell pepper
10 green olives, chopped
4 whole black peppers
4 cloves
1 teaspoon (2 g) cumin
1 tablespoon (6.2 g) cilantro or coriander seeds

amarones con Tequila

Shrimp with Tequila

6-8 large shrimp,
   butterflied
3 tablespoons (42 ml) oil
3 thin slices onion
4 peppercorns
¼ bell pepper, sliced thin
½ tomato, sliced thin
3 leaves dried oregano
1 cup (227 g) tomato
   sauce
¾ ounces (21 ml) white
   wine
1½ ounces (42 ml) tequila

MARINADE
2 cloves garlic, minced
Juice from a lime
2 tablespoons (28 ml)
   olive oil
1 sprig fresh epazote
½ teaspoon (.25 g)
   oregano
Salt
Pepper

Marinate the shrimp for ½ hour.

Meanwhile fry the onion, peppercorns, bell pepper, tomato, and oregano in oil until soft.

Add fresh tomato sauce. When it is hot, add white wine.

Add shrimp and simmer until cooked, 8-10 minutes. Add tequila during the last 30 seconds that the shrimp are cooking.

Serve with rice, carrots, chayote, and sliced onion sautéed in butter with chopped bacon.

Camarones a la Diabla

Shrimp in Red Sauce

Prepare the chiles as in fish in red sauce.

Fry the shrimp in butter for about 3 minutes. Salt to taste. Mix all of the other ingredients together and pour over the shrimp. Heat.

1 pound (.5 kg) shrimp, peeled

2 tablespoons (30 ml) juice of sour orange, or if unavailable 3 parts orange to one part lime can be substituted

12-15 chiles *de árbol*, seeds and stems removed

3 tablespoons (43 g) butter

2 tablespoons (28 g) catsup

2 tablespoons (28 g) tomato sauce

1 teaspoon (5 g) Worcestershire sauce

Salt to taste

Pescado a la Diabla

Fish in Red Sauce

1 whole fish, 1½ pounds
  (¾ kg)
2 limes
3 garlic cloves
12-15 dried chiles *de árbol,*
  seeds and stems
  removed
1½ cups (355 ml) cooking
  oil
2 tablespoons (28 g)
  catsup
1 teaspoon (5 ml)
  Worcestershire sauce

Many varieties of fish, both whole and filleted, are used for this. The following is for a whole fish.

Cut about 4 evenly-spaced diagonal slits along each side of the fish. Squeeze the juice of 1 lime on both sides of the fish. Put the pulp from the garlic evenly in the slits. Salt both sides of fish. (Or, make a paste with a *molcajete* or blender, using the garlic, salt, and the juice from about ½ lime. Put the paste evenly in the slits.) Allow to marinate about 25-30 minutes.

Heat the chiles in a dry frying pan for about 15 minutes over moderate heat, turning so that both sides are dark, but not burned. Put the chiles into enough water to float them, and let them soak about 20 minutes. Either blend them in a *molcajete* with about cup of the water (about 5 minutes) or in a blender. Strain, mashing the juice out. It should be a reddish coffee-colored liquid that's fairly hot.

Dry the fish, get the oil quite hot, and gently put the fish in. It should cook until it's a light brown, 10 or more minutes on each side.

All the other ingredients should be mixed with the liquid from the chiles and poured over the fish. Add water, if necessary, to make a thick sauce, and heat.

Camarones Aquario

Shrimp Aquarius

Sauté bell pepper in the butter for 5 minutes. Add the onion and sauté until nearly tender.

Add shrimp, salt, and sauté for about 6-8 minutes.

Mix the cream, stock, and Worcestershire sauce together. Add ham strips and heat. Pour cream sauce over shrimp and serve.

1 bell pepper, sliced into
   strips
2 tablespoons (30 g)
   butter
3 thin slices onion, cut
   crossways twice
8 large shrimp
Salt
3 tablespoons (42 ml)
   cream
1 tablespoon (14 ml)
   chicken stock
¼ teaspoon (1.5 g)
Worcestershire sauce
8 strips of ham, sliced thin

Camarones Frito

Fried Shrimp

Separate eggs and beat whites until fluffy. Stir in yolks. Mix with beer, flour, baking powder, and salt.

Dip shrimp in mixture, and fry in ¾ inch (3 cm) hot oil for 5 minutes or until golden.

2 eggs
6 ounces (177 ml) beer
½ cup (113 g) flour
1 tablespoon (14 g) baking
   powder
Salt
Oil
1 pound (.5 kg) cleaned
   shrimp

Jaibas Rellenas Chelém

Stuffed Crab

2 fish heads or any part of fish for stock
½ teaspoon (1 g) oregano
3 bay leaves
Salt and pepper
1 pound (.5 kg) minced crab meat
2 tablespoons (30 ml) cooking oil
1 onion, chopped
3 tablespoons (43 g) raisins
2 tablespoons (28 g) capers
15 seedless green olives, chopped
3 cloves garlic, minced
1 teaspoon (3.3 g) thyme
3 tablespoons (44 ml) vinegar
6-12 crab shells
7 tomatoes, chopped
1 sweet chile, chopped
1 chile *xcatic,* chopped
2 *habanero* chiles, chopped
1 tablespoon (15 ml) olive oil
3 tablespoons (43 g) flour
2 tablespoons (30 ml) white wine or vinegar
1 apple, chopped (optional)
1 teaspoon (5 g) sugar

Boil fish ½ hour in 1 quart or more of water with oregano, bay leaves, salt and pepper. Strain.

Fry crab in oil with half the onion, raisins, capers (be careful of the salt), olives, garlic, thyme, salt, pepper, and vinegar for 10 minutes.

Stuff the crab shells with this mixture.

To make the sauce, fry the tomatoes, half the onion, and all the chiles for 15 minutes until everything is soft. Stir in the olive oil at the end. If it is too thick to be a sauce, stir in a little fish stock.

Add about 3 tablespoons (45 g) flour to stock. Heat, stirring, until it thickens.

To serve, put some stock in a deep plate. Put the crab in the stock, and spoon the sauce over the crab.

Crepas de Jaiba Endiabladas

Deviled Crab Crêpes

Simmer the celery and onion in butter or oil until soft.

Add the flour, mustard, parsley, Worcestershire sauce, pinch of salt, hot sauce, and milk. Cook over a low fire, stirring until it thickens.

Beat an egg and mix well with the sauce. Cook about 4 minutes and then stir the crab in. Put the crab mixture in crêpes that have been kept warm, roll up, and serve.

Marcela said that when she serves crab crêpes, she serves the sauces on the side so that people can choose which to put on their crêpes. The sauce is the same to begin with, then she adds other ingredients.

1 stalk celery, finely chopped
½ onion, finely chopped
2 tablespoons (28 g) butter
2 tablespoons (28 g) flour
1½ tablespoons (21 g) prepared mustard
1 tablespoon (4 g) chopped parsley
Salt
1½ teaspoons (7 g) Worcestershire sauce
Dash of bottled hot sauce such as Tabasco
1 cup (236 ml) milk
1 egg
1 cup minced crab meat (about ½ pound) (224 g, ¼ kg)

Salsas de Crepas Jaibas

Sauce for Crab Crêpes

2 tablespoons (28 g)
  butter
2 tablespoons (28 g) flour
¼ teaspoon (1⅛ g) salt
½ cup (118 ml) half and
  half
2 egg yolks
½ cup (118 ml) chicken
  broth
2 tablespoons (16 g)
  shredded gruyere
  cheese
1 tablespoon (14 g) dry
  sherry

Heat the butter. Gradually stir in flour and salt. Add half and half, stirring constantly.

Beat the egg yolks, mix with a little of the sauce, and stir it into the rest of the sauce. Add gruyere cheese, and stir until smooth. Add dry sherry and stir.

For another sauce use Chihuahua cheese and omit the sherry.

Caserola de Jaiba y Tallarín

Crab and Noodle Casserole

Roast chiles over the burner for about 5 minutes, turning until blistered all over. Wrap in a wet dish towel for 10 minutes. Peel, devein, and cut into strips.

Put half of the cooked noodles in the bottom of a greased baking dish. Distribute the crab over the noodles. Dot with half the butter, and salt lightly. Put the rest of the noodles over the top. Dot with the remaining butter, and distribute the cheese and half and half. Place the chile strips around the top, and bake in a 300°(150°C) oven for 15 to 20 minutes.

2 green chiles, not very hot
Cooked noodles
½ pound (224 g, ¼ kg) crab meat
2 ounces *Chihuahua* cheese and 2 ounces *Oaxaca* cheese, shredded (56 g of each)
1½ tablespoons (21 g) butter
½ cup (110 ml) half and half
Salt

Jaibas Rellenas con Chilmole

Stuffed Crab with Blackened Chile Sauce

½ pound (¼ kg) ground pork
3 cloves, ground
⅛ teaspoon (.5 g) cinnamon
Salt and pepper
6 tomatoes, chopped
1 onion, chopped
½ bell pepper, chopped
1 pound (.5 kg) crab meat
1 egg, beaten
Crab shells
Flour
Oil
12 olives, chopped
3½ ounces (1, 100-g package) *chilmole (relleno negro)*

Make a *picadillo* of the ground pork: brown it with the clove, cinnamon, salt and pepper, chopping and stirring to keep the meat separated and crumbly.

Add 3 tomatoes, the onion, and the bell pepper. Simmer covered over low heat for 30 minutes, stirring frequently.

Add the crab meat and beaten egg and mix. Stuff the shells. Sprinkle the tops with flour.

For the sauce, fry the remaining tomatoes, half the onion, and the olives in oil for 10 minutes.

Stir 3 tablespoons (45 g) flour into 2 quarts water. Heat a little water separately. Add *chilmole* and stir until it is smooth. Add this to the 2 quarts (2 l) water. Bring to a boil, stirring. Turn flame down so that it is simmering.

Add crabs and simmer for 15 minutes. Put crabs on a platter and cover with the sauce.

Chilpachole de Jaibas

Crab Meat with Chiles

Prepare chiles as in Jaibas Rellenas con Chilmole (previous recipe). Blend garlic, onions, and chiles in a little water from the chiles, or grind in a *molcajete,* chiles first.

Boil fish head with *epazote* in 2 quarts (2 l) or more of salted water for 20 minutes.

Add all the other ingredients and simmer for 10 minutes.

7 *ancho* chiles
3 cloves garlic
2 onions
1 fish head or other pieces
1 sprig *epazote*
¾ pound (340 g) crab meat
1 tablespoon (15 g) Maggi
   sauce
Salt

Langosta Capeada

Batter Fried Lobster

1 lime
Meat of one lobster tail
1 cup (227 g) flour
1 teaspoon (5 g) baking
   powder
1 egg
Salt
Oil to cover half of lobster

Squeeze lime juice on lobster and let sit a few minutes. Dip lobster in flour that has been mixed with baking powder. Dip in egg that has been beaten with salt.

Place in hot oil and fry about 5 minutes on each side.

Lobster al Mojo de Ajo

Lobster with Butter and Garlic

4 lobster tails, boiled 3
   minutes
12 (or more) garlic cloves,
   crushed
¼ to ⅓ cup (56-75 ml) olive
Oil
Salt

Slit lobster tails open. Distribute crushed garlic into the slits, generously. (This is a recipe to indulge a taste for garlic.) Sauté the lobster tails in the oil until the garlic gets soft, about 15 minutes. Salt to taste.

Pulpo con Tomate

Octopus with Tomatoes

Boil octopus with ½ onion, garlic, bay leaf, and herbs for about 2 hours.

If it is a large one, peel octopus when it is done. The skin can be gelatinous, especially on a large octopus. Cut octopus in pieces. Fry tomatoes, remaining onion, and olives in oil for 10 minutes. Add the octopus and simmer 5 minutes. Served with rice. Sometimes it is served as a *botana*.

2 pounds (1 kg) octopus
2 onions, chopped
2 cloves garlic
1 bay leaf
¼ teaspoon (1 g) thyme
¼ teaspoon (1 g) marjoram
8 tomatoes, chopped
15 olives, chopped
3 tablespoons (44 ml) oil
Salt

Seviche de Pulpo Frito

Deep Fried Octopus Seviche

Deep-fry octopus in hot oil for about 5 minutes. Remove from oil and let cool.

Cut into bite-sized pieces and mix with all the other ingredients. Can be served as part of a meal or as a *botana*.

1½ pounds (680 g)
  octopus
Oil
1 onion, chopped
1 tomato, chopped
1 *habanero* chile, chopped
Cilantro, chopped
1 lime
Salt
Pepper

Empanizado

Breaded and Fried Small Barracuda

1 barracuda or other fish
about 16 inches (41 cm)
long
Salt
Pepper
Juice of 2 limes
2 cloves garlic, minced
Bread crumbs
Egg, beaten
Oil

Marinate fish in salt, pepper, lime juice, and garlic for 2 hours. Dip in bread crumbs, egg, and again in bread crumbs.

Fry in hot oil for 5 minutes.

# ALBERTO

Alberto Castillo was born in 1920. He acts like he was born later, which is encouraging. He makes getting old seem not like the end of the world. His interest in the world is that of a young person.

Alberto is one-quarter pirate. His maternal grandmother was a Yucatec Maya from Campeche, a Gulf Coast port that had long been targeted by pirate attacks. Surrounding the city was a fortressed wall built in the seventeenth century to protect the residents. The wall was successful at least some of the time. During his grandmother's youth, a group of pirates caught during a raid were imprisoned in Campeche, and upon their release, Alberto's grandmother found one to marry. If "ladies love outlaws," she must have been one of them or in a big hurry to get married. The two had a girl child who grew up and married a man from Mérida—a mestizo with a lot of Spanish blood. Alberto was born of this union.

He is also a product of Mérida in its heyday. The city he grew up in was wealthy, aristocratic, and permeated by European culture. As a result of all these influences, Alberto has a genteel demeanor and offbeat sense of humor. He lives alone in the house his parents bought when he was eight years old. There his major occupations are painting pictures and rearranging rooms.

Alberto spends a great deal of time revamping his house. One day he showed me a sink he had built in what was, at the time, the dining room. The base of the sink was constructed to look like a remnant from a Maya ruin. To the untrained eye, it did. And it went well with the 200-year-old wall it appeared to be a part of. Another day he pointed out a drain he had installed in the tile floor near what was then the dining room table. When I asked why he didn't simply patch the roof, he explained, "It is easier to work on the floor than on the roof."

La Casa Alberto

I have heard numerous comments about Alberto's house. One was: "Alberto doesn't live in a house. It's got its own charm—the way he has it decorated with his paintings and sculptures all over the place—but it's not really a house. It's a shed."

Another was: "There are so many mosquitoes in Alberto's house that you might as well be sitting out in the jungle. I don't know how he can stand it. He says they don't bother him, but he swats at them just like everybody else."

The following remarks came from a woman who lives in Gringo Gulch and tends to say unkind things. "We all just love Alberto, but I don't see how he can live like that. His house reminds me of the Adams Family. How many light sockets does it have . . . one? Why, then, are there wires dangling all over the house? They're conducting electricity, you know; the wires are live. He makes connections out of any old wires he happens to have."

"It's amazing he hasn't electrocuted himself. You know that little room he calls 'the bar'? Right after building that room, he had a few of us over for lunch in it. Well, it started raining, and water began dripping on my hair. I wrapped a towel around my head but didn't say a word about what was happening. Finally, when the towel was soaking wet, I said, 'Doesn't that leak bother you?' Alberto replied, 'Only when it rains.' Finally after our feet were soaking wet, he suggested, 'Maybe we should go into the other room.'"

"Perhaps it's good that the house is so dark—you can't see the cobwebs hanging from everything. Those chandeliers he makes out of beads and shells and God-knows-what-all-else look like they haven't been cleaned in a hundred years."

At least some of these observations are based on the truth. A visitor can think they are in a room and, looking around more closely, realize they are not officially in a room—they are partly outside. One day Alberto and I were finishing a lunch of bell peppers stuffed with ground fish smothered with a tomato sauce, in addition to rice and refried beans. It began raining very hard. At first only two trickles were coming through anywhere near us, and they were next to each other, easy to keep an eye on.

"Do you want me to put a pot or something under that?" I asked when water had begun to drip on my shoulder. Then I noticed that my letter on the table was getting wet.

"No there's just that one," Alberto replied, looking up and pointing to the original leak. Right away, a drop hit him in the eye. He took off his glasses and wiped his eye, moved his chair out of the rain, and looked up again. "Maybe I need a whole new roof," he said with seldom-heard resignation.

The Adams Family analogy is appropriate. As Alberto was putting on his apron to make lunch one afternoon, he began laughing. A scorpion had run out of his apron pocket. A few weeks earlier, a scorpion had stung him while he was reaching for a pot in the kitchen. He has been stung so many times that he regards the venomous arachnids as little more than a minor irritant. He thinks he has acquired an immunity to their sting.

Alberto is one of the nicest individuals I have known. He never has anything extremely nasty to say about anyone. In addition to his optimistic attitude, he speaks about nearly everything in the same tone of voice, stopping just short of excitement.

Among his favorite subjects is the ten years he lived in Acapulco, from 1954 to 1964. He calls them Acapulco's "golden years" and his "decade of sin." Describing this period of his life one evening, Alberto began telling me how he and his wife used to collect oysters and eat them on the beach. They would walk from the *zócalo* to Condessa Beach with oyster knives, limes, and a bottle of hot sauce. Then they would have beer at Coleta Beach. He went on to tell me that years later he developed thrombosis in his eyes, after which he was blind for a week. That experience rendered in his inimitable style sounded almost as enjoyable as walking the beaches of Acapulco.

Alberto now wears tinted glasses because his eyes have become sensitive to light. Yet the manner in which he walks through his house often gives the impression that he may be blind; he touches surfaces as if to verify where he is. When you look at his paintings, however, you realize that he sees quite well.

Mexico City

Alberto left Mérida in 1942, when he was twenty-two years old. His dream was to live in Mexico's exciting capital, Mexico City, which he had visited two years earlier. His departure went practically unannounced.

He sold his guitar and bicycle and bought a ticket for the boat to Veracruz. When he told his mother he had the ticket and was going to Mexico City, she was horrified. Setting off to find his father at work, he told him as well. "Be careful" were his father's only words. Upon Alberto's return home, his mother asked when he would be going.

"Now," Alberto said, and later that day he left a crying mother on the Progreso pier. From Veracruz he took the train to Mexico City, where he was to remain for twelve years.

Alberto had grown up with an interest in art. His father had drawn as a hobby, so Alberto arrived in Mexico City determined to study the visual arts. At first he enrolled in an oil painting class at the Academia San Carlos. Then he saw Diego Rivera doing a fresco and was fascinated enough to also sign up for a fresco class he was teaching.

Very soon Alberto developed an interest in cooking as well and registered for a class at the Mexico School of Gastronomy. Each weekend the students in his class prepared a dinner in the culinary style they had been studying. The final weekend was to be different: the teacher himself, Agustín Aragón Leyva, would be preparing the meal. Agustín told his students that the gathering would be a gala affair. The menu, he said, would be a surprise.

When the final weekend of class arrived, Agustín went to a house where cats that had been raised to be eaten were sold. He purchased four of the animals to take home and cook up for the festive event.

Present at this long-awaited dinner were students, their wives, and two distinguished guests. One was Alma Reed, a writer from the United States who had decided to stay in Mexico after leaving her lover, Felipe Carrillo Puerto, governor of the state of Yucatán. After her departure, Puerto had allegedly hired a composer and lyricist to write a song about her. The outgrowth of this creative effort, a song entitled "The Pilgrim" was written. It became known throughout all of Mexico. Puerto, a champion of the poor, was later assassinated. Reed went on to write a biography of José Clemente Orozco, one of the great Mexican muralists. Upon her death she was buried beside Puerto in Mérida.

The other distinguished guest was Ana Gabriela Mistral, a renowned poet and educator who was born in Chile. Publication of her first book *Desolación* had been subsidized in part by a group of New York teachers in 1922. She was awarded the Nobel Prize for Literature in 1945.

Alberto, his wife, and Agustín were the only people who knew what they were eating, but everyone thought it was good. When everyone had finished eating, Agustín let his guests in on the surprise. I would have expected a poet to be the last one to behave this way, but it was Ana who ran from the table to let the cat out of the bag, so to speak.

Cat, for Agustín, was a once-in-a-lifetime event. He taught his students to prepare rose petal salad and other dishes made with flowers. He was not only a professor of gastronomy but an admirer of the work of Frédéric Chopin, and he was a pianist in his own right. Married to a Maya woman named Josefina Che, he accompanied her while she—donning a *huipil*, the traditional Maya dress, adorned with sequins—sang and recited Yucatecan poetry in Mexico City.

Alberto met many celebrities during his stay in the capital. Among those he came to know well were his fresco teacher Diego Rivera and his artist-wife Frida Kahlo; by all accounts, the two did not always have a happy relationship. For one thing, they both had affairs. Diego's, according to Alberto, came first; Frida's, which followed, seemed to involve Communists such as Leon Trotsky and David Siqueiros, who, like Diego, was one of Mexico's famous muralists. For another, the couple argued endlessly. Their fights were well documented around town.

To keep some semblance of peace, the couple lived in separate houses next door to each other. That way, says Alberto, they could be together when they wanted to and apart while having an affair or a fight. Sometimes when Frida was separated from Diego, she needed money desperately and would sell her paintings for as little as 300 pesos, the equivalent of about fifty dollars. Diego did not always value his work either. One time when Alberto was at Diego's house, the muralist started sketching.

"He kept crumpling his drawings and throwing them in the wastebasket," Alberto explained. Then he added, "I wish I had taken them out."

I once asked Alberto if Diego Rivera was upset when his wife died.

"Oh, yes," Alberto replied. "He felt very bad. He really loved Frida."

We humans sometimes have strange ways of showing our love.

Acapulco

When Alberto went to Acapulco in 1954, he rented a building to use as an art studio. It was across the street from Armando's, one of the "in" restaurants in town. "If you missed Armando's, you missed Acapulco," as Alberto puts it. Previously, Armando had been a waiter at La Perla, the restaurant at *La Quebrada,* where the spectaculer dives are made. There he met Lana Turner, and she helped finance the opening of his restaurant.

At night, Alberto would convert his studio into a restaurant. He was able to seat people at six tables, and with his canvases covering the walls, people had an opportunity while dining to choose a painting to buy. Armando often came to Alberto's restaurant in search of "a change in cooking and atmosphere." Sometimes he would walk right up to Alberto and say loud enough for everyone present to hear, "Hey, Picasso, you have to come over and meet Brigitte Bardot!" or "Hey, Picasso, come over and meet Debbie Reynolds!"

When asked what he did with the leftovers at his restaurant, Alberto says "There never were leftovers." Every night he made a soup, a salad, and four entrees—one each of pork, chicken, beef, and fish. Some of the most popular dishes he served were seviche Acapulco style (p. 13), seviche with coconut milk (p. 14), two different avocado soups (p. 45), fish and shrimp casserole (p. 180), fried shrimp (p. 193), chicken with pineapple and orange juice (p. 145), chicken with pineappple (p. 146), chicken-filled pineapple (p. 147), and baked chicken with cambray onions (p. 148)—a recipe he adopted from a German woman who had been a cook for Queen Mary while she was in France.

Acapulco in the fifties and sixties was a haven for well-known people. Merle Oberon, an actress from the United States who had become an art collector and expatriot living in Acapulco, occasionally stopped by Alberto's studio to chat or to invite him to a party. Most often they talked about art and animals. Whenever she visited, she brought along her two German shepherds on a leash. And since Alberto had two ocelots in his studio, they would take their animals for a walk on the beach. In Alberto's case, he would walk and they would ride, one on each of his shoulders.

Invitations to parties were ongoing. Alberto says that for a while he attended three to five parties every night after closing his restaurant. Then he became friends with a wealthy Bacardi distributor who offered to sponsor his first art showing. Bacardi supplied the drinks. After the showing, the two men went to a party. There Alberto became very tired and could no longer dance. Someone took him upstairs, put powder to his nose, and told him to sniff.

"I felt fine after that," he says. "I felt wide awake, like I had had nothing to drink. So I had two more drinks and said, 'Uh-oh, never again.' After that, people would call me for parties, but I always said no."

Three years after moving to Acapulco, Alberto's wife died suddenly of a liver ailment at the age of thirty-five. Losing her was hard on him. "I'll never get married again," Alberto told himself, and he didn't.

"There were too many women in Acapulco. Many women came to visit from the United States every year. Once, three of my girlfriends came at the same time."

I asked what he did.

"I had to tell one of them about the others; she said no problem. The other two, well, they just thought I was painting too much."

Ohio

A couple who owned a restaurant in Ohio came to Acapulco every winter. Each time, they invited Alberto to return with them and work as a bartender in their restaurant. He eventually did and spent several years in Ohio. He arrived there with some clothes, painting supplies, a kilo of dried chiles, and a kilo of *masa.*

Alberto was familiar with two plants he saw growing wild in Ohio— *cuitlacoche* and *epazote*—neither of which, he was to learn, were considered fit for human consumption in that part of the world. One day while walking past a cornfield with some friends, he saw some *cuitlacoche,* a corn-fungus that grows around kernels of corn in rainy seasons.

"How do you cook it here?" he asked his companions.

They looked at him as though he were crazy and said they fed it to the cows. They did not believe him when he said it was also good for people.

To prove his point, Alberto made quesadillas of *cuitlacoche* for his friends. He scraped the kernels of fungus off the cob and sautéed them in a little oil for 8 minutes. (The fungus can also be boiled in water to cover for 10 minutes.) Next he put about 1 tablespoon of Parmesan cheese and 1 tablespoon of the sautéed *cuitlacoche* on a corn tortilla, folded it, and heated it in about ⅛ inch of oil, turning the tortilla until the cheese melted.

The Ohioans, unlike the cows, finally had a choice about what to do with fungus-infested corn. It did not take long for many of them to become *cuitlacoche* aficionados.

Back to Mérida

When Alberto left Ohio to move back to Mérida, he had with him two suit-cases, a television set, and a few other commodities he had bought in the United States. In one of the suitcases were two new suits. His trip went well, but his belongings never made it to Mérida.

In speaking of things such as witches in southern Mexico, one is less likely to be looked upon as weird than in the United States. The fantastic is mainstream. Soon after his return home, his friend Lucy decided to visit a *brujo,* a male witch. She wanted him to cast a spell that would stop her husband from having an extramarital affair. Alberto accompanied her.

The *brujo* failed at his mission, and Lucy eventually got divorced; but in other respects the man proved quite impressive. He burned some copal and read the smoke. He told Alberto that his luggage had been stolen at the airport in the United States. (No one had said a word to the *brujo* about the missing luggage.) Thinking back, Alberto remembered that the last time he had seen his bags, a man was pushing them in a cart at the airport. The *brujo* then told Alberto that if he returned immediately, he could get his belongings back. Deciding not to make the long journey to Cleveland, Alberto gave up on his luggage.

About six years later, Alberto was visiting friends in Ohio. One afternoon while on the outskirts of Cleveland, he went to a pawnshop, as he is often inclined to do. There he saw his two suits—they were hanging together near a couple of his shirts. He bought the suits.

Upon Alberto's return to Mérida this time, his niece went to the same *brujo* to help cure her of an ailment. He would have some medicine ready for her in a few days, he told her. Several days later she heard a knock at her door. It was the *brujo,* coming to deliver the medicine.

Not having the money to pay for it, she asked if she could take it to him the next day. She did, but upon arriving at the *brujo*'s house, she was told that he was dead, that he had died the week before.

When Alberto finished telling me this story, I asked him if he believed in *brujos.*

"I do now," he answered.

Alberto's house in Mérida, like his studio in Acapulco years before, doubled as a restaurant. This one was run by reservation only. Six times a week Alberto would prepare dinner for between ten and fifty people. Everyone was served the same meal. He asked what they wanted and from what country. Sometimes it was French; other times it was Italian, German, Greek, or Hawaiian. His only culinary rule was no Yucatecan food. He had grown up with it, made it for himself, but did not want to serve it in his restaurant.

Alberto's restaurant became fairly well known in the greater Mérida area. People from many walks of life dined there, often traveling from miles around. And according to the guest register, which is replete with comments on the uniqueness of the evening, Alberto's patrons had a good time. Some had such a good time that they were not allowed back. One night, for example, a guest fell in love with a large stuffed mock jaguar Alberto had made out of rags and jaguar-colored cloth. In the morning, he found a pair of panty hose in his rainforest-like backyard. People who behaved in such ways were not permitted to return.

The meals themselves were entirely homemade and often exotic. Alberto usually served paté before dinner and chutney with dinner. Specialties included *sopa de lima* (p. 44)—an exception to his culinary rule—*puerco royal* (royal pork) (p. 110), *puerco al horno con ciruelas, pasas, y crema* (pork with prune sauce) (p. 117), cold *guanábana* pudding (p. 214), cantaloupe tart (p. 215), and grape salad (p. 64).

Alberto no longer runs his restaurant. Even so, he keeps himself too busy to tend to such essentials as visiting the double lot he has owned since 1982. The lot is on a pristine beach just outside of Celestún, about fifty-five miles west of Mérida.

Celestún is a fishing village I had stopped at with a friend in 1972 while driving home to California from Mérida. Pulling out of town, we had found a sandy tire-track road that led to the beach. It was too hot to sleep on our camp cots, so we sat up all night and listened to American music drifting in on the radio from Florida, Alabama, or Louisiana across the Gulf of Mexico. The following day, we returned to Celestún, went to a restaurant-bar, and ordered a beer. The waiter brought us not only beer but one plate of octopus *seviche* and another of shrimp *seviche*. The seafood had been marinated in lime juice and was served with chopped onion, tomato, and *habanero* chile. This was my introduction to afternoon *botanas*. My fear of "the amoeba" believed to reside in uncooked vegetables, rinsed in impure water—a fear my friend had instilled in me—became secondary to the temptation aroused by the food.

When Alberto mentioned that he had not been to Celestún to pay his property tax for three years, I drove him there. On the way, he told me that the last time he had visited his property, he found his coconut trees had been cut down "just for getting to the coconuts." This time he discovered that someone had started building a concrete block house that intruded two meters onto his land. The house was about half finished, work had stopped long ago, and it was falling apart. What a surprise I had when we arrived at his lot. He had bought his property ten years after my friend and I had stayed there on the beach—small world.

After paying his tax, Alberto and I went to a restaurant in Celestún where we enjoyed a good laugh. We ordered *sopa campechana* (p. 54) and the house specialty, *tortas de jaiba y camarones*. While waiting for our soup, I showed Alberto two recipes I had been given by a restaurant employee in Puerto Escondido, Oaxaca. One was for cream of carrot soup. Although it was for a large pot, the ingredients were out of proportion.

Alberto looked at the recipe and frowned. "One kilo of butter and a kilo of flour!" he said, reading the list of ingredients. "What do you stir it with—an outboard motor?" The other recipe was for a chicken dish for eight people. It called for one chicken. "The soup is served with a hammer and chisel, and the chicken with a toothpick," he went on. "And who's the cook," he asked, "Jesus?"

Alberto keeps himself busy all the time. If he is not painting canvases with oils, renovating, remodeling, or repairing things, he is immersed in short-term projects of one sort or another. Stopping in to see him one day, I was greeted with unexpected news: he had just finished making us each a pair of pants from some material he had found lying around his house. The blue and white fabric was most likely intended for window drapery or curtains. The pants have their own charm.

I use Alberto as a model for the amount of energy I would like to have if and when I make it to seventy-six.

FRUTAS y POSTRES

Desserts in Mexico, as in most of Latin America, are quite simple. There is such a variety of delicious fruits that simple recipes can be easily adapted and the fruit alone finishes a meal satisfactorily.

Sueño Maya
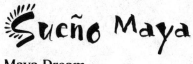

Maya Dream

1 cup (225 ml) coffee (not
  too strong)
Twist of lemon and orange
2, 2-inch (5¾ cm) sticks
  cinnamon
3 or 4 drops vanilla
Honey to taste
Tequila

Simmer all together for 8 to 10 minutes. Strain. Add ¾ ounce
(21 ml) tequila.

Served with *Xtabentun* (a liqueur) on the side.

Budín de Guanábana

Guanábana Pudding

Meat from 1 *guanábana*
3 eggs
1 can sweetened
  condensed milk
3 tablespoons (45 g) corn
  flour

Alberto makes simple desserts from tropical fruits that are very
good.

Blend all together. Cook, stirring until thick. Chill in individual
dishes before serving.

The same can be done with 4 bananas, canned or fresh mangos, and other fruits.

Pay de Melón

Cantaloupe Tart

To make vanilla sugar, place a vanilla bean in powdered sugar for several days. Vanilla flavoring can also be used at the time of making it.

Sift flour into bowl with salt. Cut shortening into little pieces, and mix into flour until they look like peas. Sprinkle a little water over mixture in the bowl, and toss lightly. Repeat until water is gone.

Gather the dough and shape into a ball. Flatten the dough into a 4-5 inch (10-13 cm) round, cover with plastic wrap and chill for 1 hour. Preheat oven to 400° (205°C).

Roll out the dough to fit a 9-inch (23 cm) tart pan with a removable bottom and trim off the extra dough. Put this in the freezer for 15 minutes. Line the dough with a piece of aluminum foil and fill with dry beans. Bake the tart shell for 10–12 minutes, until set. Remove the beans and the foil and continue to bake until the shell is a golden brown, 8–10 minutes more.

For the filling, scoop the meat out of the cantaloupe using a melon baller. Simmer the apricot preserves for 2 minutes, and gently brush over crust. Place cantaloupe balls close together over the preserves.

Sprinkle with vanilla and sugar, and refrigerate 1 hour.

CRUST
1½ cups (210 g) flour
1 teaspoon (6.2 g) salt
6 tablespoons (90 g) cold shortening
4 tablespoons (56 ml) ice water, or more if necessary

FILLING
1 large cantaloupe
1 jar of apricot preserves
½ cup (112 g) vanilla sugar

Pay de Mango

Mango Tart

3 large mangos (or a large
   can)
4 tablespoons (56 g) corn
   starch
3 eggs
1 tablespoon (15 ml)
   vanilla
1 can sweetened
   condensed milk
Graham crackers or corn
   flakes
Whipped cream

Blend a few slices of mango with the corn starch, eggs, vanilla, and milk. Sprinkle crumbled graham crackers or corn flakes in a pie plate, adding a little water or melted butter to make it coherent. Spread it around the plate so that it forms a crust. Pour the blended mixture over the crust, and put the remaining mango slices on top.

Top with whipped cream and refrigerate. Virtually any fruit can be used—apricot, apple, guava, banana, papaya, *guanábana,* or coconut.

(If fresh coconut is used, shred and cook 20 minutes, adding sugar to taste.)

Mango Mousse

1 can mangos or fresh
   mangos (sugar is added
         with fresh)
1 can sweetened
   condensed milk
Whipped cream

Blend mangos and condensed milk, top with whipped cream, and refrigerate.

Bolitas de Naranja

Orange Balls

Extract juice from carrots in a juice extractor.

Squeeze the juice from the pulp (the juice is not a part of the recipe) and put pulp in a pan with the condensed milk, orange peel, and orange juice.

Mix well, and beat over low flame, without stirring, until it thickens.

When it is almost dry, remove from heat and let cool.

Make little balls, and roll them in sugar. Refrigerate

2 pounds (1 kg) carrots
1 can sweetened
**   condensed milk**
1 tablespoon (14 g)
**   orange peel**
6 ounces (180 ml) orange
**   juice**
Sugar to taste

Bolitas de Zanahorias

Coconut and Carrot Balls

Peel carrots and boil them until tender. Drain and blend with sugar, orange juice, and half the coconut. (Juice of carrot is not used.)

Make balls of the mixture and roll them in the remaining coconut. Refrigerate until cold.

½ pound (¼ kg) carrots
½ pound (¼ kg) grated
**   coconut**
½ pound (¼ kg) sugar
Juice of one orange

Pastel de Calabacitas

Squash Cake

½ pound (¼ kg) butter
½ cup (35 g) sugar
4 eggs
½ pound (225 g) flour
2 teaspoons (15 g) baking powder
14 ounces (400 g) canned sweetened condensed milk
1 pound (450 g) zucchini, sliced
5 tablespoons (75 g) raisins
2 cups (320 g) candied fruit or dried fruit
2 cups (450 ml) whipping cream

Mix the butter with sugar until creamy. Beat eggs into butter, one at a time. Sift in flour, baking powder, and add milk, beating the whole time. Add the squash, raisins, and fruit.

Put half in one cake mold, and half in another. Bake in a 392° (200°C) oven for 35 or 40 minutes.

Cool and put one half on a plate. Top with the cream, whipped, and then the other half of the cake. If you only have one cake mold, the whole thing can be baked, and then sliced in half to add the whipped cream filling.

Cover the top with whipped cream. Add candied fruit if desired.

Licuados

Blended Fruit Drinks

Licuados are very popular in the Yucatán. They are served almost any time of the day because they are refreshing and cool. Fruits such as cantaloupe, bananas, pineapple, papaya, and mangos are blended with ice, water, and sometimes a little milk. A raw egg can be added. The ingredients are whipped in a blender until the drink has the thickness of a milk shake.

A *licuado* can also be made by blending raw *chaya,* ice, water, lemon juice or lime juice, and sugar to taste.

Frutas

List of Tropical Fruits

Some fruits common to the Yucatán are *aoramuyo, anona, caymeto,* egg tree fruit from Costa Rica, *guanábana, guayaba, mamey, nancy, pitahsya,* sour orange, and *zapote.*

Where To Find It
Sources for Southwestern Ingredients

ARIZONA

Phoenix Area

Carol Steele Co., 7303 E. Indian School Rd., Scottsdale, AZ 85251; 602-947-4596

El Molino, 117 S. 22nd St., Phoenix, AZ 85304; 602-241-0364

Estrella Tortilla Factory and Deli, 1004 S. Central Ave., Phoenix, AZ 85003; 602-253-5947

Flores Bakery, 8402 S. Avenida del Yaqui, Guadalupe, AZ 85283; 602-831-9709

La Tolteca, 609 E. Washington, Phoenix, AZ 85004; 602-253-1511

Mercado Mexico, 8212 S. Avenida del Yaqui, Guadalupe, AZ 85283; 602-831-5925

Mi Ranchito Mexican Food Products, 3217 W. McDowell Rd., Phoenix, AZ 85009; 602-272-3949

Native Seeds/Search, 2509 N. Campbell Ave. #325, Tucson, AZ 85719

CALIFORNIA

Fresno

Chihuahua Inc., 1435 Fresno St., Fresno, CA 93706; P.O. Box 12304, Fresno, CA 93777; 209-266-9964

Chihuahua Tortilleria, 718 F St., Fresno, CA 93706

Los Angeles Area

Central Market, Broadway (downtown), Los Angeles, CA; 213-749-0645

Cotija Cheese Co., 15130 Nelson Ave., City of Industry, CA 91744; 818-968-2284 (wholesale cheese)

El Mercado, First Ave. and Lorena, Los Angeles, CA 90063; 213-268-3451

La Luz del Dia, 624 N. Main (near Sunset), Los Angeles, CA; 213-972-9578

Liborio Market, 864 S. Vermont Ave. (near 9th), Los Angeles, CA; 213-386-1458

Los Cinco Puntos, 3300 Brooklyn Ave., East Los Angeles, CA; 213-261-4084

Mercado Cali Mex, 2377 Pico Blvd. (near Vermont), Los Angeles, CA; 213-384-9387

Peter Pan Market, 2791 Pico Blvd. (near Normandie), Los Angeles, CA; 213-737-3595

Tianguis supermarkets.
3610 North Peak Rd., El Monte, CA; 818-443-0498
1201 Westwood Air Blvd., Montebello, CA 90640
7300 N. Atlantic, Cudahay, CA

Modesto

Don Juan Foods, 1715 Crows Landing Rd., Modesto, CA 95351; 209-538-0817

Oakland

Mi Rancho, 464 7th St., Oakland, CA 94607; 415-451-2393

Redwood City

Mario's Food Market, 2835 Middlefield Rd., Redwood City, CA 94063; 415-364-9524

Mission Bell Bakery, 2526 Middlefield Rd., Redwood City, CA 94063; 415-365-7001

Sacramento

Casa Grande, 1730 Broadway, Sacramento, CA 95818; 916-443-5039

Farmer's Market on Franklin Blvd. and La Esperanza Mexican Bakery next door (916-455-0215)

Jalisco, 318 12th St., Sacramento, CA; 916-448-3175

La Hacienda, 5029 Franklin, Sacramento, CA; 916-452-2352

Maxis Supermarket, 5814 Stockton Rd., Sacramento, CA; 916-452-6661

Salinas

Sal-Rex Foods, 258 Griffin St., Salinas, CA 93901

San Diego Area

Casa Magui, S.A., Av. Constitucion 932, Tijuana, B.C., Mexico; 5-7086

El Indio Shop, 3695 India St., San Diego, CA 92103; 714-299-0333

El Nopalito Tortilla Factory, 560 Santa Fe Dr., Encinitas, CA 92024; 714-436-5775

Fruteria Jacaranda, Stand 90, Interior Mercado, Tijuana, B.C., Mexico

Main market (Revolucion), Tijuana, B.C., Mexico

Woo Chee Chong, 633 16th St., San Diego, CA 91001; 714-233-6311

San Francisco

Casa Lucas Market, 2934 24th St., San Francisco, CA 94110; 415-826-4334

Casa Sanchez, 2778 24th St., San Francisco, CA 94110; 415-282-2400

La Favorita, 2977 24th St., San Francisco, CA 94110

La Tapatia Tortilleria, 411 Grand Ave., South, San Francisco, CA 94080; 415-489-5881

La Palma, 2884 24th St., San Francisco, CA 94110; 415-648-5500

Latin American Imports, 3403 Mission Ave., San Francisco, CA 94110; 415-648-0844

Mi Rancho Market, 3365 20th St., San Francisco, CA 94110; 415-647-0580

San Jose

Cal-Foods, 195 S. 28th St., San Jose, CA 95116; 408-292-4296

Santa Ana

El Toro, 1340 W. 1st St., Santa Ana, CA 92703; 714-836-1393

Potato Bin Rancho Market, 1605 West St., Santa Ana, CA 92703; 714-547-8497

Santa Barbara

La Tolteca, 614 E. Haley St., Santa Barbara, CA 93101; 805-963-0847

Santa Cruz Market, 605 N. Milpas St., Santa Barbara, CA 93101

Villareal Market, 728 E. Haley St., Santa Barbara, CA 93101; 805-963-2613

COLORADO

Denver

Casa Herrera, 2049 Larimer St., Denver, CO 80205

El Molino Foods, 1078 Santa Fe Dr., Denver, CO 80204; 303-623-7870

El Progreso, 2282 Broadway (near corner at Larimer), Denver, CO 80205; 303-623-0576

Johnnie's Market, 2030 Larimer St., Denver, CO 80205; 303-297-0155

Safeway Supermarket, 2660 Federal Blvd., Denver, CO 80219; 303-477-5091

CONNECTICUT

Gilbertie's Herb Gardens, Sylvan Ln., Westport, CT 06880; 203-277-4175

Hay Day, 907 Post Rd. E., Westport, CT 06880; 203-227-4258

GEORGIA

Atlanta

Rinconcito Latino, Ansley Square Mall, 1492B Piedmont Ave. NE, Atlanta, GA 30309; 912-874-3724

ILLINOIS

Chicago

El Pelicano, 1911 S. Blue Island Ave., Chicago, IL 60608; 312-226-4743

La Casa del Pueblo, 1810 S. Blue Island Ave., Chicago, IL 60608; 312-421-4640

La Unica, 1515 W. Devon Ave., Chicago, IL 60660; 312-274-7788

Supermercado del Rey, 1714 W. 18th St., Chicago, IL 60608; 312-738-1817

KENTUCKY

Louisville

Abrigo Oriental Foods, 423 W. Chestnut St., Louisville, KY 40202; 502-584-4909

Mendoza Mexican Grocery, 4608 Gravois Ave., Louisville, KY; 505-353-9955

MASSACHUSETTS

Boston Area

Garcia Superette, 367 Centre Ave., Jamaica Plain, MA 02130; 617-524-1521

Harbar Corporation, 30 Germania St., Jamaica Plain, MA 02130; 617-524-6107

India Tea & Spice Inc., 9-B Cushing Ave., Cushing Square, Belmont, MA 02178; 617-484-3737

Ricardo y Maria's Tortillas, 30 Germania St., Jamaica Plain, MA 02130; 617-524-6107

Star Market, 625 Mt. Auburn St., Cambridge, MA 02128; 617-491-3000

Stop and Shop, 390 D St., East Boston, MA 02128; 617-463-7000

MICHIGAN

Detroit

Algo Especial, 2628 Bagley, Detroit, MI 48216; 313-963-9013

La Colmena Supermercado, Bagley at 17th St., Detroit, MI 48216; 313-237-0295

La Jalisciense, 2634 Bagley, Detroit, MI 48216; 313-237-0008

MINNESOTA

St. Paul

El Burrito Mexican Foods, 196 Concord Ave., St. Paul, MN; 612-227-2192

Joseph's Food Market, 736 Oakdale Ave., St. Paul, MN 55107

La Tortilleria Coronado, 197 Concord, St. Paul, MN; 612-292-1988

Morgan's Mexican Lebanese Foods, 736 S. Robert St., St. Paul, MN; 612-291-2955

MISSOURI

St. Louis

Soulard Market, 730 Carroll St., St. Louis, MO; 314-421-2008

Tropicana Market, 5001 Lindenwood, St. Louis, MO; 314-353-7326

NEW MEXICO

Santa Fe and Area

Embudo Smokehouse, P.O. Box 154, Embudo, NM 87531; 800-852-4707

La Carreta, Box 70, Dixon, NM 87527; 505-579-4358

Leona's de Chimayo, P.O. Box 579, Chimayo, NM 87522; 800-4LEONAS

Pastores Lamb, P.O. Box 118, Los Ojos, NM 87551; 800-321-5262

Rancho Casados, P.O. Box 1149, San Juan Pueblo, NM 87566; 505-852-4482

Santa Fe School of Cooking Market, 116 W. San Francisco St., Santa Fe, NM 87501; 505-983-4511

Sweetwoods Dairy, P.O. Box 1238 Peña Blanca, NM 87041; 505-465-2608

Theo. Roybal Store, Rear 212, 214, 216 Galisteo St., Santa Fe, NM 87501

NEW YORK

New York City and Vicinity

Midtown

International Groceries and Meat Market, 529 9th Ave. (between 39th and 40th Streets), New York, NY 10018; 212-279-5514

Latin American Products, 142 West 46th St., New York, NY 10036; 212-302-4323

Downtown

Pete's Spice, 174 1st Ave., New York, NY 10009; 212-254-8773

Trinacria Importing Co., 415 3rd Ave., New York, NY 10016; 212-532-5567

Uptown (East)

La Marqueta, Park Ave. between 112th and 116th Streets, New York, NY

Uptown (West)

Hummingbird Foods and Spices, 2520 Broadway, New York, NY 10025

Latin American Grocery, 2585 Broadway, New York, NY 10025

New York Vicinity

L. A. Barbone Inc., 170 W. Main St., Goshen, NY 10924; 914-294-9711

Laraia's Cheese Co., Nanuet, NY 10954; 914-627-2070

OHIO

Cincinnati

Bolti's Market, 1801 Vine, Cincinnati, OH 45210; 513-579-1721

Cleveland

Danny Boy Farm Market, 24579 Lorain Rd., Cleveland, OH; 216-777-2338

La Borincana Foods Inc., 2127 Fulton Rd., Cleveland, OH 44113; 216-651-2351

Rico Imported Latin Foods, 4506 Lorain, Cleveland, OH 44102; 216-961-4993

OKLAHOMA

Oklahoma City

Mayphe's International Foods, 7519 N. May Ave., Oklahoma, OK 73116; 405-848-2002

OREGON

Portland

Corno & Son, 711 S.E. Union Ave., Portland, OR 97214

PENNSYLVANIA

Philadelphia and Area

J&J Food Imports, 1014 Federal St., Philadelphia, PA 19147; 215-334-0914

La Cantina, 6140 Brockton Rd., Hatboro, PA 19040; 215-487-1360

TEXAS

Brownsville

The Mexican Kitchen, P.O. Box 214,
Brownsville, TX 78520; 512-544-6028

Dallas

Danal's Stockyards Stores
        4800 Columbia Ave., Dallas, TX
75219; 214-821-2934
        10544 Harry Hines, Dallas, TX 75220;
214-357-0241
        5011 Lemmon Ave., Dallas, TX
75209; 214-528-8570

Hernandez Mexican Foods, 2120 Alamo St.,
Dallas, TX 75202; 214-742-2533

Horticultural Enterprises, P.O. Box 34082,
Dallas, TX 75234

Super Mercado Mexico
501 S. Rosemont Ave., Dallas, TX; 214-941-
6293
2008 Greenville Ave., Dallas, TX; 214-821-
0171
1235 S. Buckner Blvd., Dallas, TX; 214-391-
5831
5535 Columbia Ave., Dallas, TX; 214-698-9986
1314 W. Davis St., Dallas, TX; 214-924-1225

Fort Worth

Danal's Stockyards Store, 2469 N. Houston,
Ft. Worth, TX 76106

Houston

Antone's Import Co., 807 Taft, 8111 South
Main, and 1639 South Voss Rd., Houston, TX

Mexicatessen, 302 W. Crosstimbers, Houston,

TX 77018; 713-691-2010
Rice Food Market, 3700 Navigation Blvd.,
Houston, TX 77003

Manchaca

It's About Thyme, P.O. Box 878, Manchaca, TX
78652; 512-280-1192

San Antonio

Alamo Masa, 1603 N. Laredo, San Antonio, TX
78209

Chicago Tortilleria, 2009 Blanco, San Antonio,
TX

El Mercado, San Antonio, TX

Frank Pizzini, 202 Produce Row, San Antonio,
TX 78207; 512-227-2082

H.E.B. Food Stores, 4821 Broadway, San
Antonio, TX

WASHINGTON

Seattle and Area

El Mercado Latino, 1514 Pike Pl., Seattle, WA
98101; 206-623-3240

El Ranchito, 1313 E. 1st Ave., Zillah, WA
98953
Herb Farm, 32804 Issaquah, Fall City Rd., Fall
City, WA 98024

Sanchez Mexican Grocery, 1914 Pike Place
Market, Seattle, WA 98104; 206-682-2822

Wapato

Krueger Pepper Gardens, Rt. 1, Box 1086-C,
Wapato, WA 98951; 509-877-3677

WASHINGTON, D.C. AREA

Americana Grocery, 1813 Columbia Rd. NW, Washington, DC 20009; 202-265-7455

Arlington Bodega, 6017 N. Wilson Blvd., Arlington, VA 22205; 703-532-6849

Bethesda Ave. Co-op, 4937 Bethesda Ave., Bethesda, MD 20014; 301-986-0796

Casa Lebrato, 1729 Columbia Rd. NW, Washington, DC; 202-234-0099

Casa Pena, 1636 17th St. NW, Washington, DC 20009; 202-462-2222

Safeway, 1747 Columbia Rd. NW, Washington, DC 20009; 202-667-0774

WISCONSIN

Milwaukee

Casa Martinez, 605 S. 5th St., Milwaukee, WI 53204

CANADA

ALBERTA

Calgary

Lori's Gourmet Delikatessen, 314 10th St. NW, Calgary, AB, Canada T2N 1V8; 403-270-4464

BRITISH COLUMBIA

Vancouver

Que Pasa Mexican Foods, 530 W. 17th Ave., Vancouver, BC, Canada V5Z 1T4; 604-874-0064

Victoria

Las Flores Restaurant, 536 Yates St., Victoria, BC; 604-386-6313

ONTARIO

Ottawa

El Mexicano Food Products, Ltd., 285-A St. Patrick St., Ottawa, ON, Canada KIN 5K4; 613-238-2391; 613-224-9870

Toronto

Dinah's Cupboard, 9 Yorkville Ave., Toronto, ON, Canada

El Capricho Espanol, 312 College St., Toronto, ON, Canada; 416-967-6582

El Sol de Espana, College St. at Ossington, Toronto, ON, Canada

Home of the Gourmet, 550 Yonge St., Toronto, ON, Canada; 416-921-2823

New Portuguese Fish Store, Augusta St., Toronto, ON, Canada

Sanci Fruit Company, 66 Kensington Ave., Toronto, ON, Canada; 416-368-6541

Wong Yung's, 187 Dundas St. W., Toronto, ON, Canada; 416-368-3555

Index